The Football Agent

Knut Høibraaten

ISBN: **8269009903**
ISBN-13: **978-8269009903**

To *my lovely teenager princess Julie.* When *you are allowed to read this book, after your 18th birthday, I hope you will forgive your dear father. May you inherit all my spirit of adventure, but only half of my madness.*

CONTENTS

IMPORTANT INFORMATION TO THE READER

Dear, wonderful Reader!

First, thank you so much for buying my book. And if you didn't buy it, but borrowed it or stole it, thank you anyway for reading it. I sincerely hope you will thank me when you have finished it – because you liked it, not in a "thank God it's finally over" kind of way.

I wasn't able to find any book about being a football agent that was actually written by a football agent. And that's definitely not due to a lack of material; most agents have loads of stories to tell. It's probably because most of us can hardly write our own names. I don't exactly have a PhD in literature either, but I love to tell a good story, and now I am going to tell you this one. Not that I am one of the big sharks in the world of agents either. To be honest, I am more like a herring. However, I still have plenty of stories to tell.

As a reader, there are a couple of things you should know before you start. No part of this book is fiction – everything is factual and from real life!

This book has one major source: myself. I communicate stories, events and situations the way I experienced them. From my point of view. Other people involved may of course have their own, entirely different views and opinions about this.

Anyway, my publisher and editor have insisted that everything in this book must be reliable. To achieve this, I was forced to anonymize a little. Therefore, the text isn't as straightforward as it could have been, since I had to try to balance on the right side of the law. My claims and opinions aren't objective truths no matter how you view them, but they are definitely mine. The key elements in the book, the story itself and the main events and issues are all 100% truthful. Enjoy!

ROSENBORG BALLKLUB – LA LA LA LA LA LA LA LA LA LA LA LA

It was the best of times, it was the worst of times, it was the age of wisdom, it was the age of foolishness ...
— Charles Dickens, A Tale of Two Cities

Norwegian football in the beginning of the 2000s. Times were good. Sponsorship money, new stadium projects. Steeply increasing player salaries and transfer and agent fees. Money was pouring into Norwegian football clubs, at least on the paper, through promises of sponsor contracts projected years ahead from a multitude of growth companies. Financing was made though heavily geared loans that financial institutions generated at a rate which would put Saruman's orc production to shame. And the money poured out as well, but then in solid cash. A shaky foundation.

When the party was going strong, early 2006, I did my first player transfer. Through some random events and a cheeky phone call to Rune Bratseth in Rosenborg, my opportunity presented itself. The Trondheim club, renowned for its faithful fans cheering their home team to the tune of Pippi Longstockings, then filled my pockets with 25 thousand pounds. Selling football players was easy as pie! This was definitely my kind of business! I was going to clear the table in this game going forward.

At this moment in time, my Internet company had recently

1

gone bankrupt, and at the same time, I was going through a divorce. My creditors were all over me, and – to put it mildly – life sucked. I had no idea what to do next, and felt like I didn't have much left to lose. For some reason I remembered a Chinese saying that went something like *Choose a job you love, and you will never have to work again.* With this in the back of my head, at the lowest point in my life so far, I asked myself; what do I really love? Where is my passion so deep that I can work with something without considering it work? The answer came right away: Football.

Since the time I was an alley cat in the capital of Western Norway – Bergen – football and my home team Brann have always generated the deepest and most passionate emotions in me. Brann Stadion and my tribal brother fans there had occupied a large part of my heart for as long as I can remember. But how the heck could I use that passion to earn any money? I could not become a football player – that career stranded like a whale on Brann's junior team. Firstly, I just wasn't good enough, and secondly I loved beer and women just that little bit too much, so my coach put me on the reserve team and kept punishing me with long runs in the dark valley of Isdalen.

So the athletics department was off the table. On the other hand, I had great skills as a salesman and relations builder. After all, before I messed it up, I had built a successful company from zero to a client list counting more than a thousand names. I excelled at sales, and I loved football. The answer was to become a football agent.

As I already mentioned, there was a football bonanza in Norway, and the clubs spent money more or less indiscriminately. Moreover I had a network on Balkan through my father who lived there. Balkan was overflowing with young talents streaming out to big and small clubs throughout Europe.

In the autumn of 2005, I arranged for the young jewel Jahmir Hyka to try out for Rosenborg. After a new try-out in the beginning of 2006, Rosenborg signed a three-year contract for Hyka. I made money. Nevertheless, Rosenborg had to let him go after just one year, due to NFF's (Football Association of Norway) quotas for foreign players at that time. Hyka went on to Olympiakos, Mainz 05 and now Luzern, plus the All-Albania team. Albania's Messi and my Messiah.

The day I signed the contract with Rosenborg Ballklub and

Rune Bratseth, I was so ecstatic that I needed company to celebrate it. I was alone in "the moustache city" Trondheim, but I got a prompt response from my childhood friend Erlend, who arrived with the next plane from Bergen.

Two noisy guys from Bergen ended up in one of the traditional pubs in the city. The regulars were deeply rooted in their chairs and gave us sceptical glances when we entered the place. In general, peace and love is not the first thing that leaps to hard-boiled Trondheimers' minds when they meet big-mouthed natives from the capital of Western Norway. If Norway once become a dictatorship under a trueborn inner-valley Trondheimer with a small moustache, people from Bergen will probably be on the top of their ethnic cleansing list.

However, this night the Trondheimers would observe a physically fascinating specimen of the Western Norwegian. You see, Erlend is not the small and quiet type. He towers 211 centimetres above the ground with his shoes off. After ten minutes of more or less inhaling Sambuca, Erlend jerked his head up as the local hero Åge Aleksandersen's tune *Rio de Janeiro* blew out from the speakers. He climbed up on the nearest table, with all his height, and cranked up an exhilarated version of the folk dance parody The Støveldance, originally performed by the characters Hansi, Günther and Fritz in the Christmas TV comedy *The Julekalender*. The wary regulars lowered their shoulders and started laughing and applauding. After all, in the TV show, Hansi and his crew are from the Trondheim area. The crowd cheered. And the Sambuca had started to give value for the money, including very visible changes in my face. My doctor once said that it's probably caused by one or more episodes in my youth of large consumption of alcohol in a short time. My body has developed almost an allergy against alcohol. When I drink something strong quickly, I sometimes get a reddish-purple rash in my face and down my neck. So I must have been quite a show myself, sitting in a corner with my flaming alcohol rash screaming with laughter at Erlend's dance show.

Early next morning my phone rang. It was 100% teetotaller Rune Bratseth. He told me to show up at Rosenborg's stadium Lerkendal immediately to sign an extra document. The concept hangover shakes got a new meaning. I jumped into a cab, in my stained suit with matching creased shirt, and almost whispered *Lerkendal, please*, secretly hoping that the driver wouldn't hear me and maybe take me somewhere else. But in vain.

I arrived at "Brakka", Rosenborg's cosy administration building, pale and moist from increasing trepidation. That day I learned the quick and brutal way that a football transfer also includes solid doses of hard work, diplomacy between clubs and associations both home and abroad, and a meticulously accurate filling-in of a number of documents, before it's *really* a done deal. Bratseth had years' of experience, and he was nice enough to guide me through the various stages of this process. The most important thing I learned after a few hours with Rune, was that in this business you definitely don't sell any bear's skin before the beast has been both killed, skinned and cut up.

From nature, I am equipped with 50/50 of wisdom and madness, so in the Norwegian football business at that time I was among equals. My first transfer was officially a done deal, and I had made good money. Quickly. That whetted my appetite for more, and it was the start of my career as a football agent. Next on my to-do list was to become an official player agent with a FIFA license. The sooner the better.

I immediately put myself on the case.

BOOGIE ON THE BALKANS

SK Brann from Bergen is the football club of my heart. I was born and grew up not far from their stadium – Brann Stadion – and as mentioned I played in Brann until I became a junior player. Going to a Brann match in my youth was always a something I looked forward to. I usually went with Erlend, later known as the table-dancing entertainer in Trondheim. At that time, he lived one floor below me. We went down to the main road, where we joined the flow of supporters walking in from downtown. People from Bergen, and especially Brann supporters, are eternal optimists. Regardless of our team's standing, we were all 100% certain that today – *today* – the visiting rednecks were in for a beating. Walking towards the stadium like this we felt local patriotism swelling. A sense of community and identity was created for a lifetime. We felt like an army going to the war.

We usually arrived at the stadium and the infamous standing area – Store Stå – an hour before the match started. That gave us plenty of time to put our bodies, heads and vocal cords in the right mode before the referee's whistle sounded. We greeted our players with chants and songs when they came out for warmup, and we mocked the opposing team. The legendary speaker of Brann Stadion, Terje Bøe, always came running over the field towards us to get the atmosphere going, and each time he finished with a handstand and received deafening cheers from the crowd.

I have always pitied those who say that football is just *"22 men on a grass field running after a ball."* In my opinion, these people lack something important in their lives. For a man in Norway, there is no better place to unleash your inner chaos. On a football match, it's ok for complete strangers to hang around each other's necks and cry. The most absurd abuse can be shouted to opponents, referees and others. The fact that everybody does the same things, creates a strong sense of shared identity. The red team colour out there on the field is our time warrior suit against hostile tribes. The colour itself and the players wearing it represent each and everyone in the crowd, the street you are from, the building you live in or other aspects of what you are. They fight for you out there, and we win or lose together. It's powerful. Men who love football get a free therapy session every fortnight when there is a match. Afterwards all your psychological debris and inner tensions are gone. The clubs should charge more for their tickets.

I have never quite understood how some people can have the same strong feelings about a team from another part of the country, or even a foreign team. Your heart should belong to one team and one team only, and that should be the team from your hometown, where your identity lies. You can like the playing style of an Italian team, or the quality of English or Dutch football. Nevertheless, how someone manages to have the same feelings for a foreign team as we had and have for Brann, both impresses and puzzles me.

Rosenborg's coach, Nils Arne Eggen, said it well when he was asked about his opinion on Solskjær's manager job in Cardiff: "*I usually don't say much about things that I don't know anything about. I assume Ole Gunnar has thought it through. I'm not very engaged in English football – it's mostly the kids who care about that*".

The times we couldn't afford a ticket to the live match, Erlend and I usually listened to the match on the local radio. It was pure ear candy to listen to the mad reporter Arild, who was a familiar sight on all the matches, running up and down the touchline with a backpack radio transmitter and a hairy mic in his hand. He always wore a quilted jacket – winter or summer – together with his flowing grey mane. He was so intensely engaged when he did radio reporting, that an average throw-in could sound like a 100% goal chance – with a high falsetto and an extreme talking pace even for a guy from Bergen.

He often ended up crashing into a linesman when he was following a breakthrough along the edge, yelling and screaming.

Some days when we listened to a match on the radio, especially with the floodlight matches in the autumn, Erlend and I would go out on the small balcony outside the living room in my mom's flat on the second floor. From there we could see the lights from the stadium flowing out in the drizzle. Moreover, if the wind was right, we could hear the roaring of the crowd all the way home to our balcony, where we sat close together under a grey blanket my mother kept there for those occasions.

My parents divorced when I was four, in 1981, and I don't remember much before that. In 1993, my dad moved to Albania to start a ferry company. The next year, in 1994, I lived alone with my mother after my brother had moved out. I was 16, and my grades from Tanks College were rapidly declining. My mother became fed up of my living off the fat of the land, so she and my dad agreed to send me to Albania to get some decency into the ruffian they had put into this world. So I went to Albania. I worked there for a year, learned about life. And I spent a lot of time in Albania during the next years.

Two years later my dad was engaged in starting a football team in the capital Tirana. His formula was as follows: he hired the All-Albania coach team, and named the club Ilir Viking FC. The first part of the name, *Ilir*, came from the Illyrians – the ancient Balkan/Albanian tribes who were infamous for plundering and raping their neighbours. Together with *Viking*, our Nordic ancestors with similar proficiencies, the stage was set. The only thing lacking now was players. That was resolved with a gigantic audition, or try-out. My dad and the coach team invited hundreds of the best 14-year olds from all of Albania to a week's training camp in Tirana.

To make a long story short, the experienced and able coaches picked twenty of the most talented players, and created the very first team squad for Ilir Viking FC. Dad, always the idealist, bled money. I was asked to secure participation in Norway Cup – the annual international youth football tournament in Oslo – and to get sponsors. This was my first involvement in the football business, although on the lower end of things. I managed to get Norway's largest newspaper Aftenposten as main sponsor, and the team played their way through the cup in Oslo in 1995. It was an adventure.

The result was a goal difference of 54-0, and the team beat my beloved SK Brann 6–0 in the final on Ullevaal Stadion, in front of hundreds of ecstatic Albanians, most of them seeking asylum in Norway.

Gradually Ilir Viking FC became several age-divided teams, and they won a number of great cups in Italy and France. They also did well in the Albanian league. To my father's great sorrow, the team was discontinued around the millennium, and the players were free to go to other clubs. Several of them ended up in Greece, Switzerland, Austria, and even one in the Italian Serie A.

The craziest experience I had with Ilir Viking was during Norway Cup in 1997. Since 1993, my dad had vouched for visas for many Albanians going to Norway, both business partners, friends and some years even players participating in Norway Cup. All his guarantees were good, and there had never been any problems. Therefore, my dad's word weighed heavier and heavier in the foreign ministry. He was a man of his word, no doubt about it!

In 1997, the players were lodged in Helsfyr Primary School. The tournament had gone relatively well, and the last night we were attending a farewell dinner with the players and team leaders in a Macedonian restaurant in the Grønland part of Oslo. I was responsible for the team during the stay, and there was a good atmosphere during the dinner. There was a Macedonians-only night in the restaurant. Even though "we" were Albanians and the restaurant owners Macedonians, they considered themselves as one people. Way back, they were both parts of Greater Albania, and even today, large parts of the populations in Macedonia, Montenegro, Greece and Italy are Albanians.

Close to midnight, the goalkeeper's coach went back to Helsfyr with the players. The plane back to Tirana was scheduled to leave early next morning, so we had to get the boys packed and ready, and to bed. The other coaches and I were invited for a drink in an Albanian underground club. It was an illegal club a block from Youngstorget, behind tinted glass on the first floor. In one end, there were a mini casino with roulette and a poker table. A real table with a real dealer. In the other end, a bar and a small stage with a stripping pole.

I recognised many of the faces there from the people who had watched our matches on Ekeberg earlier that week. Handshakes and nods. Everyone had come to greet us that night. Nice. It was 4 am before I was home and in bed, well soaked. I had organised a bus ride from Helsfyr the next morning, and the lads managed this fine on their own. They were used to travelling by now. Therefore, my plan was to get up around the same time they were scheduled to land in Tirana, late afternoon the next day. It had been a tiresome week with long days.

I was staying in my dad's place in Ullevålsveien. He stayed there too, but he had other things going than Norway Cup, so he had just dropped by a couple of times to watch a few matches.

Dad's loud and angry voice woke me up abruptly. He repeated himself several times:

– *They are gone! Shit! They're fucking gone! Knut, get out of bed now! Don't you understand how serious this is?*

I didn't understand a thing. A few minutes past 5 a.m., I had hardly slept at all. In addition, the alcohol disoriented me. He grabbed my arm and yelled a few more curses, then quickly left for the living room. I jumped out of bed, into my boxers, and ran after him. He was pacing back and forth in the living room talking frenetically on the phone, and at the same time trying to put a shirt on, still in his underwear. The flat was on the second floor, just beside the house where the paparazzis had a photo orgy taking shots of Mette-Marit and Haakon – Crown Princess and Crown Prince of Norway. We had two large living rooms facing the street, with sliding doors between them. Dad marched back and forth between the two opposite walls raging into the phone.

He hung up, and I got a quick summary. Nine players had split from the school a few hours ago, with some adult men in three cars. The remaining boys claimed they knew nothing about what had happened. They had already been subjected to several "interrogations" by their coaches, and maintained that they were just as surprised as the rest of us about what had happened. Dad didn't buy it. He got the names of the players who hadn't run away, and called the father of one of them in Albania. Dad had never taken any classes in Albanian, but learned the language relatively fluently through practice. The player's father was told to call his son to explain the seriousness of the situation. A few minutes later one of the coaches called. Sure enough, after a strict call from his father in Albania, one of the boys had put the cards on the table. It turned out that our worst-case scenario had played out. Some time ago, the boys on the team were contacted by an Albanian living in

Sweden, and a plan had started to form. The players were promised work and residency in Norway. However, the real future planned for them was as illegal immigrants running errands for the Albanian mafia, in sharp contrast to the golden promises they had been lured into believing.

Dad became, if possible, even more desperate. He knew it was just a matter of hours before the nine boys were outside our reach and lost. All the players had known the escape plans, but about half of them had chosen not to run away. They weren't in any trouble as long as they promised to keep quiet. Unless...

The boy who had let down his guard and told us about it, also gave us a Norwegian mobile phone number. It was to the guy who had planned the whole thing. No name.

Dad called the number, but it went straight to an answering machine. He left a message and called once more. Answering machine again, new message. He told the machine loudly and clearly what would happen if they didn't call him back right away. It was close to six, and in a half hour a bus would be here to take the boys from the school to the airport. The plane was scheduled to take off from Fornebu airport around 9 a.m. Zürich was the first of two stopovers.

The bus arrived, picked up what remained of our team, and headed for the airport. Around the same time, the phone rang: it was the guy. Dad lectured him up and down, and ordered him to take the nine boys to the airport immediately. The guy in the other end laughed scornfully. That didn't exactly calm the old man down. The verbal war escalated with increasing threats and promises of reprisals shooting both ways. Nothing seemed to put the other guy off balance, and I could feel my father's despair. Dad is probably the nicest person on this planet, and he is ready to do anything for the ones he loves. I could practically see the movie playing inside his head about the incredibly bad prospects that lay ahead for these nine boys. It was painful.

My dad's big heart usually gains him deep respect from the people he meets. And he has met many people. When I fly with him, he'll be on familiar terms with half the cabin by the time we land. A great personality.

Now that heart was bleeding, and he was completely at a loss. I saw his eyes go black in response to something from the other end of the phone. The yelling stopped, and he continued with a low, calm voice:

– *Don't think you are the first one to threaten my life! Do you have any idea who you are talking to?*

The guy on the other end got my father's name, but it didn't ring any bells. So my dad told him to ask around in his network before he decided about whether or not to let the boys go. They hung up.

Twenty minutes later one of the coaches called enthusiastically. Their bus had just arrived at Fornebu airport, and outside the terminal the nine missing boys were waiting for them, with long faces.

Apparently the guy had talked to someone to whom my dad's name *did* ring a bell, and then made a wise decision.

I had almost forgotten all about this guy, until I saw his name in the major headlines of every newspaper in the spring of 2004. He was one of the prime suspects of the NOKAS robbery in Stavanger, which included the murder of a police officer.

This whole incident was an important experience of the dark side of football, especially since my career as an agent was in its infancy.

ONLY A HUMAN BEING CAN BE AN AGENT

As soon as I had made the decision to become a football agent, I started researching what the job entailed, and equally important, what it took to become an official agent. I knew practically nothing about it, apart from what I had picked up in the media when names of Norwegian agents like Rune Hauge and Per A. Flod came up in connection with high-profile player transfers out of Norway. I also knew that one of dad's friends, Gunnar-Martin Kjenner, worked as an agent now and then, especially for Egil "Drillo" Olsen, former manager for the Norwegian team.

Therefore, I called Kjenner to learn more. Kjenner mainly works as a lawyer, but he knew the game and explained the basic rules to me.

To be able to represent a player in contract negotiations, one of three conditions must be met:

1: If you are a close relative of the player, either in an up-down direction (mother, father, possibly uncle) or sideways (brother, sister), you are allowed to negotiate contracts according to FIFA's regulations. In addition, the Football Association of Norway is bound by FIFA's regulations in this area.

2: Anyone who is a licensed lawyer in Norway, can act as a player's agent and participate in negotiations.

3: You must be an approved player's agent, officially called Player's agent with a license from The Football Association of Norway.

However, Kjenner failed to inform me about the fourth option:

4: You just ignore the three points above, and you will in fact have a much better chance of succeeding as an agent. I will get back to this.

In 2006, I only knew about the three first options. I wasn't a licensed lawyer, and I wasn't closely related to any top players. Option 3 was the obvious choice for me, so I needed to find out how to become an official Player's agent licensed by the Football Association of Norway (NFF).

I called the Association and they told me to visit their website, where I should be able to find an easy explanation for everything. NFF's *simple* explanation of how to become a licensed player's agent, is a long torrent of babble, which I will spare you. Feel free, however, to visit the Association's website and read the whole thing. In any case, here is a summary:

....

General

Only a human being can be licensed as a player's agent.

The exam is normally arranged twice a year – in the end of March and September, respectively.

License as a player's agent is issued by the football association in the country where the person is a citizen. If the person has several nationalities, the last granted nationality should apply. If the person has had a permanent place of residence during the last two years in a country other than the one where he/she is a citizen, the association in this country is responsible for issuing the license.

In the application, the applicant must confirm that he/she has not been convicted by any official authorities or … is not under investigation by law enforcement authorities nor by any sports associations.

By filing an application, the candidate accepts to be bound by NFF's and FIFA's regulations, policies and decisions.

The agent exam

The exams are marked immediately after the last candidate has handed in their paper.

If the candidate fails the exam

A candidate who fails the exam at their third attempt, must wait two calendar years before he/she can apply to retake the exam.

....

If you are one of those who skipped the above, or if you are left with big question marks after reading the full text on the

Association's web pages, it can be summarized quickly as follows:

The only thing you *don't* need in order to become a player's agent, is to qualify for the 100 metres breaststroke at the Olympic Games.

I read carefully through the football association's instructions – word for word, sentence for sentence. I requested a certificate of good conduct from the police, and started to count the days I had been abroad during the last year. I concluded that I had been outside the border for just over the magic six months. And in that case – considering that I had been in Albania, Croatia, Montenegro, Italy, Serbia, Bosnia, Macedonia, Greece, Kosovo, Sweden plus a week on a charter trip to Egypt – which of these countries should I apply for player's agent license from? Would simply switching my nationality be simpler?

After considerable counting and calculation, it turned out to be less than six months after all. I used the neatest letter-writing layout I remembered from school, and filed my application to NFF, including various attachments. Could Yours Faithfully please be admitted to take the candidate exam for player's agents?

When I received the curriculum, my jaw dropped. It was partly in English. Even if I do have a working knowledge of English on a conversational level, I am definitely more familiar with my mother tongue. Moreover, parts of it was dry and heavy legalese. What seemed to be a never-ending listing of paragraphs with long-winded and barely understandable sentences, all of which referred to other paragraphs, and so forth and so on.

All my life I have been a quick learner, so I used to surf through school without paying much attention to homework. Until I started college, when my total lack of good study habits hit me in the face like a blind duck. I had to learn how to study, and I didn't like it one bit.

The curriculum I had received now, was without doubt the worst I had ever seen. I read page after page repeatedly, but nothing stuck in my head. I just didn't get it.

Luckily the Norwegian, and much smaller, part of the curriculum was easier to understand, even if that too was bone dry. I knew the exam consisted of 15 international questions and 15 Norwegian ones. One point for each correct answer, and you had to have 15 points to pass.

The exam date was in March 2006. The exam is conducted on

the same day, at the same time, all over the world, and only twice a year – March and September. The 15 international questions are the same for all countries, and they are kept in strict secrecy deep in FIFA's basement in Switzerland. Not until 30 minutes before the exam starts, are the questions faxed to each national football association. The secretary of the each association is the only one with access to the document, and he/she spends the minutes until the exam starts making copies of them for the candidates. The last sheet in the fax transmission from Sepp Blatter's Swiss fortress is the list of set answers.

The answer sheet is not copied, and it is strictly guarded. The sheet is not allowed to leave the body of the association's secretary until all the candidates have handed in their exam papers.

You have 90 minutes to complete the exam. Good luck!

ON WILD ROADS

My second transfer, after Jahmir Hyka to Rosenborg, was also an Albanian player. His name was Migen Memelli, and he was a striker and top scorer in the Albanian super league.

It was the end of February 2006, and I still didn't have a license to work as a football agent. I hadn't even tried to take the test. However, I had read in the local newspapers in Bergen that Brann was looking for a forward for the upcoming season.

I had to share the money I received from Hyka's transfer, with my Albanian partner, Bekim. He is a fascinating character – a man who could literally experience more on an ordinary Monday than most of us would during a lifetime. He had so many projects going on, so many phone calls in and out, and so many trips to the strangest places on this planet, that I don't know where to start describing the guy. What I can say is that he has very variable moods, from incredibly cheerful and charming to extremely dark and sinister.

In February 2006, I had only known Bekim for a few months, so I had limited experience with him. A couple of hours after I had told him about Brann's wish list, he called me to introduce Migen Memelli. At that time, Memelli played in the football club Skënderbeu from the town of Korça, far east towards Albania's border with Greece and Macedonia. The town is at a high enough altitude for it to snow there in the midwinter – a good sales pitch towards Norwegian coaches who may wonder if an Albanian is fit to play football in the Norwegian autumn and winter.

I went to Albania the next day, and drove with Bekim to Korça. The roads in Albania at that time were of a very variable standard. A heavy trafficked main road could have stretches of four-lane highway, via narrow roads with worn out oil gravel, to the other extreme, bumpy dirt roads full of holes. A Norwegian right-wing politician once claimed that Albania had better roads than Norway. It was probably not the ones on the Tirana–Elbasan–Korça route he had in mind.

This was the only road for anyone going this way – pedestrians, bicycles, cars, lorries and an unnerving number of horses with carriages. Bekim drove like a maniac, regardless of the road quality. I had my heart in my mouth for most of the drive. The worst part was in the outskirts of the city Elbasan. We half skidded around a curve way too fast, when suddenly a horse-driven carriage appeared right in front of us. Bekim barely dodged it by throwing the car out into the opposite lane — where a lorry came thundering towards us, so he had to cut right back again. By now, he had no control whatsoever over the car, and we were tearing along towards an area where people were waiting for a bus. The twenty plus people scattered in panic. But three of them didn't quite make it, and were hit by us at about thigh height. They fell and tumbled over. The rest of them crowded around our car, which had now come to a halt, and banged furiously on the windows. Bekim stepped on the gas, people jumped back, and he turned out on a field and then back on the road again. He turned to me with a deep, roaring laughter. Scary stuff.

We arrived at Korça well before the match we were there to watch. It was cold, and we booked in at a guest house with a large old open stone fireplace in the reception. Nice and warm. The match, however, which took place on a frozen, uneven grass pitch, didn't give us much opportunity to assess Memelli's abilities, or anybody else's for that matter. The players spent most of the time trying not to slip and fall.

We met with Migen after the match, talked about the possibility of try-out for Brann, and agreed that we should try to get Brann to invite him. According to FIFA's regulations, this is not allowed, since no players can talk to other clubs if they have more than six months left of their contract. Still, it's very commonplace and a generally accepted practice, in both Norway and elsewhere.

I woke up in my pension bed the next day with a crushing

hangover. Bekim gave me what was, according to him, the best remedy in the world for this – a local winter soup that is supposed to cure all kinds of bad mornings. It was unappetizing and contained some weird, slimy lumps. But I forced it down. As I was swallowing the last spoonful, my Albanian partner grinned and said:

– *Sheep's brain soup. Delicious, don't you think?*

More roars of laughter.

I called Per-Ove Ludvigsen in Brann, who I barely knew at this point, and presented Migen Memelli as the solution to their forward issue. A few days later, we agreed to let Memelli come to see Brann while they were at a training camp in La Manga, Spain. It turned out to be an unforgettable experience for several of us, especially Bekim and his sense of smell.

THE EXAM

It was time to get my own papers in order. In March, the infamous exam was finally taking place. We were 10–12 candidates; an odd group spread around small standing tables in the football association's premises on the main football stadium in Oslo, Ullevaal Stadion – also known as Ullevaal Business Class. The tables were in a wide corridor behind a row of doors leading out to various VIP lounges, where those who can pay enjoy food and drink with friends and business partners before a match. The lounges have windows from floor to ceiling, and separate doors out to the grandstand, with good seats for watching the match.

In the following years, I was going to spend a lot of time in rooms like this one, but then always with a football match going on, many people, lots of alcohol and dollar signs in my eyes.

This chilly morning, however, both the stadium and the corridors were empty. Except for the other candidates and myself, sipping coffee while the atmosphere became increasingly tense. Nobody talked. My nervousness and fear of failing increased with each heartbeat – beats so loud I could swear everyone around me could hear them. I started to sweat.

The secretary bid us a short welcome. She wore a skirt and a tight blouse, buttoned up in the way of a sexually sophisticated. Her hair was set up in a tight knot like a librarian. She disappeared quickly through a door. After a hard struggle with the curriculum from FIFA – an organization that appeared to me more and more like a dark, powerful and living organism in the style of the

Freemasons or the inner circles of the Catholic Church – this woman was the first representative of this organism that I met face to face. She reinforced my impression. I frenetically tried to place her mentally in any classic porn scene with a dominant secretary who apologises to her boss for an error she has made. It sort of worked, and I grinned and shook my head over my own twisted mind. My mental movie had just reached the mandatory blowjob, when everybody's thoughts were interrupted by the last candidate crashing through the door, ten minutes before ten. It was Jack Karadas. He is a cousin of Azar Karadas – a reasonably good forward and centre back from Eid in Nordfjord. It is said that every family has a black sheep, and according to Jack's reputation, he was the one, black as coal.

After sitting immobile as pillars of salt for twenty minutes, we were brutally jerked out of our trance. Jack spoke loudly and addressed everyone in the room with questions and statements about this and that. He caught the eye of the man by the table closest to the door where he came in, and a tirade of words accumulated to a specific question. Jack stared and waited for the man, who was a lawyer, to reply. The lawyer looked questioningly at each of us, as if to say *what the fuck just happened?* Two seconds passed, and as on cue, we all opened our mouths simultaneously to answer Jack's trivial question. Everyone noticed that everyone else too had opened their mouths, and shut up. Damned awkward! The lawyer saved the situation by answering Jack, who had wondered if we too found the curriculum difficult? He claimed that he was a lot more nervous now than he was when taking his law school exam, even if the curriculum there obviously was much more comprehensive. The difference was that the law school curriculum made sense as you learned to crack certain codes on the way, in contrast with all the scattered and incomprehensible paragraphs in the FIFA material. He had never seen anything like it. The rest of us, our hearts already pumping at max rate, sighed heavily in a joint symphony. Any shred of confidence anyone may have had before this exam, was certainly gone now.

An exam that meant everything to me. If I passed, all doors opened up. If I failed, it meant 600 euros out the window and six months to the next time I had the opportunity. And the lucrative summer window in the transfer market would be closed for me. Too much was at stake, I was stressed out, and the paragraphs blended like fifty shades of grey paint in my head.

My confidence was at rock bottom when my porn fantasy entered again on her high heels to escort us to the exam room. It was a medium sized business lounge. However, instead of a cosy long table set for a party, there were rows of small tables, like a small, rural classroom. Outside the gigantic windows there were 28,000 empty seats covered with snow. On the middle of what would become a green grass field in a couple of months, a fellow in thick coveralls strolled along with a long stick in one hand and a walkie-talkie in the other. I had no idea what he was doing, but he put the stick in the ground, spoke into the walkie-talkie, moved a few meters, stick in ground again, more talking.

We were arranged in the room in such a way that my feeble thoughts of cheating were quickly dismissed. The questions were written with small letters in bold type. They sent the assignment sheet via fax, and it exited the fax machine slanting. Then it was run through a copier, so the letters flowed into each other. Not only did we have to interpret the weird and contradictory questions FIFA had come up with, we also literally had to interpret letter for letter. When the sentences are constructed in a completely foreign way, that makes an interesting additional challenge.

On tests and exams throughout my school years, I was usually the first one to finish, so I wasn't too worried about the timing aspect. Ninety minutes should be more than enough. I worked my way through question after question, as methodically as I could, ticking off an answer for each of them. After ten questions, half-guessing each of them, my hopes were dwindling. Then this one came up. I can't recall it verbatim, but it doesn't matter too much. The point is that it went something like this:

Antonio was born on April 2nd, 1990 in Uruguay. He moved to Paraguay in 1997, and played three years on Aztek Warriors' youth team. In 1999, he was brought to a club in Uruguay, and had to move back over the border to be able to attend to training sessions. The Uruguayan club, Bangool, organized it for Antonio to live with a host family close to the club's training field and the local school. Antonio's parents remained in Paraguay. Bangool's home city is 5 kilometres from the Uruguayan border. On January 1st, 2005, Bangool wants to offer Antonio contract as a professional player. Aztek Warriors then demand education and solidarity compensation from Bangool.

Which is the correct answer?

Then came a listing of four or five loooong multiple-choice options, with minimal and barely comprehensible differences.

I have later shown this question to directors of football in both Norwegian and foreign clubs. These are people with powerful positions – positions that require a lot more knowledge than anyone would expect from a football agent. None of them knew the right answer. Most of them struggled to understand even the question.

To cut a long story short, there are other regulations in force in Latin-America than in Europe, yet others in Australia, and a completely different set in the United States (actually things are very different over there). In some countries, there are also complex rules about whether or not the player lives less than six kilometres from the neighbouring country, and if he does, a different set of criteria kick in for a potential transfer to that country. The time he has lived there, his age, this and that may or may not affect things in various directions. In addition to several other tricky paragraphs.

Therefore, I wasn't too surprised to learn, less than half an hour after completing the exam, that regrettably I had failed. Each of us could choose if we wanted to know the result there and then or via mail later. We all wanted it there and then, but the majority wanted the secretary to whisper it in their ear. Only Jack, the lawyer and I told her to say it aloud. I failed, with the score 13 of 20. The lawyer failed too, with 11 of 20. Jack, however, the black cousin, got 15 – the minimum requirement for a pass. He shouted with joy, and told us he had already failed twice, so this was his last chance in a long time.

I was one of the last ones to know the result, and the others had left one by one after having it whispered in their ears by the secretary, who by now had become stunningly sexy. I had spent the last 30 minutes of the test completing the scene on the imaginary office with the exclusive Chesterfield sofa. Now we were the only ones left in the lounge, chatting. She was a lot nicer than the impression I got at first, and my feeling of failure was fading away. I was very curious about the whispered results, and to my surprise, she shared willingly.

Everyone had failed except for Jack Karadas! I guess the misfortune of others can be a source of joy as well. I went home, not really knowing what I could do differently when preparing for my next shot at the test, in September. But I had plenty of time. If Jack Karadas had made it, I would damned well make it too! After all, I did better than the lawyer. Jack Karadas is infamous in Norwegian football, and some of the rumours about him are really crazy. One of them had enough credibility, in addition to being confirmed by several sources, to end up in countrywide newspapers in Norway. Karadas had supposedly threatened to kill Morgan Andersen, at that time playing for FC LYN. Truth be told, these are probably the two biggest clowns in Norwegian football, but on opposite extremes of the scale. Morgan is a bungler, but with good intentions. It's just that he has this unique ability to fuck up even the simplest things for himself. Thereafter he usually chooses to use a distorted version of reality as a basis for getting back on track. The result is that he always ends up looking like an idiot. Nevertheless, I think Morgan has been getting way too much heat and ill-natured comments from the press and others. As mentioned, he isn't a bad guy. Jack, on the other hand, is. He is out of control and definitely not someone you want as your enemy. So I made sure he never became one of mine.

In any case, failing the exam was a big dent in my plan. It put the whole thing in jeopardy. I had already booked several deals, and I had sent e-mails and other info to various clubs telling them about the new FIFA agent in Norway. Besides I was about to complete the Memelli deal. But in that case I was already so far into the process that it looked like it was going to go through, license or not.

STRIPPING IN LA MANGA

Not long after talking with Brann about try-out for Migen Memelli, we were standing there: the object of the sale – Migen, my unpredictable partner – Bekim, and yours truly. Around us were the facilities in La Manga, a partly closed off area consisting of a few hotels, several training fields and a small stadium with a stand on one side. The Football Association of Norway bought shares in the facilities early in the process, and all Norwegian teams – in both the Elite League and the First Division – are subsidized with a training stay in La Manga each winter. The teams spend one to two weeks here, together with other Norwegian and European teams. That way the teams get good training conditions in midwinter, and they can play training matches against other teams, including local Spanish teams from the lower divisions. Lots of reporters, talent scouts, agents and others with interests in football also show up here. It has become a nice tradition for everyone involved, with a relaxed, snug and friendly atmosphere.

The players and support staff live in a big apartment complex on the hill above the plain where the training fields are – four to six men per room. The rest are accommodated in hotels in the same area, or other places in La Manga.

It was a nice surprise to learn that we were to live together with the players. This was quite uncommon. Mons Ivar Mjelde, Brann's coach, and the Director of Football, Per-Ove Ludvigsen, received us with open arms, and I felt very much part of the club "family". We had our meals with them, participated in closed player meetings, and were escorted by the players in some small Fiats they borrow during their stay.

The days consisted of training in the morning and dead time until a second training session in the afternoon. Then shared dinner, and more dead time. This is a recipe for cabin fever, and the players were creative in coming up with activities when things started to get boring. Some played golf, others went on excursions to various places, while many spent a good deal of time playing cards. There was a total ban on alcohol, and severe punishments for anyone who didn't comply.

However, the ban didn't apply to me, so in the nights I often went to a hotel nearby where many reporters stayed. It had a bar and, equally important, a casino.

I spent two nights in the casino with Brann's Scottish players, Robbie Winters and Charlie Miller. They had snuck out of their rooms and were here on the reporters' mercy. As far as I could see, they drank just as heavily as I did, and one day when we kept it going until seven in the morning, Robbie and Charlie gave me a lift to the morning training session. Robbie drove like a mad man and we were all cheering and shouting. On the roads in this area, they have set up short but high speed bumps to make sure the speed limit of 40 kilometres per hour (25 mph) is respected. Robbie squeezed what he could out of the Fiat on all the gears, and we slammed over the bumps so hard I thought the car would fall apart. The coach, Mons Ivar Mjelde, probably understood more than he expressed when we arrived chuckling at the training field. But he didn't say anything. Robbie and Charlie were favourites of the fans in Bergen, so he looked through his fingers with this.

Migen Memelli was a monk during his stay, and presented himself solidly at the trainings. Extremely strong-bodied he excelled on the team in tests of speed and springiness conducted by the support team. A stallion of a player.

An important test that could turn out to be the decisive for a contract, was a training match against Iceland's pride, KR Reykjavik. Brann played a weak match, and it ended 1–1, but Migen played well and scored Brann's goal – beautifully.

A few hours after the match, Bekim and I were notified that Brann was very interested in signing Migen, if the total economy of the package was acceptable. Total economy in this context means transfer fee, salary per year times the length of the contract, any bonuses of various kinds and finally the agent's fee.

Bekim claimed he had spoken to Migen's club, Skënderbeu, who wanted at least 100,000 euros for Memelli. At that time, this was more than acceptable for a club like Brann, who easily had to pay the triple amount for a half-decent player from the Norwegian First Division. After a little back and forth, Migen himself was happy with a gross salary of around 80 000 euros. In other words, we reached a verbal agreement about the total package that night, and felt even more part of Brann's football family.

The next day was the last one for Brann in La Manga, and according to tradition, there was going to be an end-of-stay party where the alcohol ban was lifted with immediate effect.

This party is used each year as a teambuilding event. It is a pleasant and informal gathering with a flat structure when it comes to coach team and players. No outsiders are invited, and all reporters are ordered to stay far away. Therefore, I was very pleasantly surprised when Mons Ivar Mjelde came over to me that afternoon and invited both Bekim and me to join in. As far as Mons Ivar could recall from his years as player and coach for Brann, we were the first outsiders ever to attend. I looked very much forward to it.

We ate lovely food and had quality liquid in our glasses. The atmosphere built steadily hour for hour, up to what would turn out to be the night's big event. A memory for life.

The thing is that Brann, and probably many other clubs as well, have a rite of passage for the new players of the year that night. The new players get notice a few days in advance to prepare a performance of their own. It's up to them what they want to do. The hope is that they make an idiot of themselves in front of the rest of the team. The new players due for their baptism by fire that night, were Petter Vaagan Moen, the great talent from the club Hamarkameratene who Brann handed out a million plus euros for, Janez Zavrl, the defender from the Slovenian club NK Domžale, Dylan MacAllister, forward from Australia and last, but not least, Migen Memelli. The contract and transfer papers weren't formally signed yet, but we had shaken hands, and the rest would be relatively uncomplicated. Only trivial formalities. Or so we thought.

Petter Vaagan Moen can't have made much of an impression with his act, since I cannot even remember what he did. Janez sang something weird, with hands folded, chin to his chest, looking down at the floor, like a timid schoolgirl. It was embarrassingly lame, and the others couldn't bring themselves to bully him out of sheer compassion, which made it only more awkward and embarrassing.

The tanned surfer dude from Australia, Dylan MacAllister, was a very different story. He was going to do some sort of parlour game, and he needed an assistant. After a little back and forth, the players managed to drive Bekim up on the stage, somewhat reluctantly. He is chubby, but also looks strangely athletic. He is also shiny bald, and his face has a fierce expression in default mode. During the week, the players had got to know him as a fun guy who often made them laugh, so it was with love that they pushed him up on stage. Dylan tied a blindfold over his eyes and told him to lie down on his back. It was a guessing game for the senses.

First, he had to taste something and tell us what it was. Simple. It was a piece of mandarin. Then he should listen, and tell us what he thought he heard. Again simple. It was Dylan snapping his fingers. So far, pretty lame, but the final act was yet to come. His was going to test his sense of smell too.

Dylan pulled down his pants and boxers, and sat down straddling with his anus just above the Albanian's nose while he held his finger over his mouth to signal that everyone had to keep their mouth shut. Smothered chuckles could be heard, otherwise it was quiet.

– *Bekim, what do you smell?*

A few seconds passed, before Bekim lifted his arm up towards his head. It stopped against Dylan's underwear-tan-line pale ass. Hi jerked his torso, lifted his head straight up into the Aussie's perineum, and slapped his face against his manhood before he managed to manoeuvre himself free. He ripped off his blindfold and got up quickly. Everyone screamed with laughter. But my friend from the Balkans was furious. His eyes went black and he scolded Dylan like hell. This was below his dignity. Being an adaptable person though, and with the audience laughing hysterically, he turned the table and laughed with them, although with a false laughter. He came over to me and hissed into my ear that this was fucking not okay, that grown men shouldn't do things like this to each other. For someone born and raised in Communist and closed off Albania, this was even more offensive than it would be for the rest of us. The cheering and applauding finally died out, and it was time for the last one, Migen.

With his powerful typical Slavic jaw and chin, muscular body and a two-day beard, it was difficult to picture him captivating us with a beautiful singing voice. He didn't speak English very well, but he managed to explain that he would sing a song he had learned from his mother. It was about the warriors from his homeland of Albania, widely famous for their courage. We didn't understand the words, but he performed it with such intensity and quality that we were all spellbound. It reminded me of one of those YouTube clips with Simon Cowell, where someone comes up on stage giving a first impression that completely clashes with what comes out of their mouth. It was a great final act from the new players. At least that's what I thought. Because not long after Migen had finished his song, I saw, just too late to react, an idea being born in Mons Ivar Mjelde's eyes, across the table from where I was sitting.

– *Knut must do an act! You are new here as well. It's only fair.*

All the guys were getting well pickled, and it was getting impossible for me to slip out of this. I was pushed out on the floor, no idea what to do next. I actually like standing in front of an audience and talking, I like doing all kinds of shows, and I love applause and attention. However, I am compulsive about always being prepared, if not down to the minutest detail, then at least to some degree. Now I was standing there.

I sing like a crow, and although I have an ok sense of humour, I am never able to recall any jokes.

I ended up putting on some foxy music, worked myself up on the bar counter, and stripped down to my socks, Coyote Ugly style. It was a hit, everybody laughed.

I was initiated – one of the guys. I have always been well received on Brann Stadion after that. When I meet someone who were at the party that night, they all remember the stripping agent.

We were back in Bergen again, to sort out the last, quick formalities around Migen's transfer. Bekim turned up with a signed statement from Skënderbeu authorizing him to sign the transfer as a proxy for the club. I, as agent, together with Per-Ove from Brann and Migen, signed his personal contract.

In order to complete an international transfer successfully, three things must be in the Norwegian Football Association's hands before they give permission to play. Before that is settled, the permission to play lies with the previous club. We had signed the personal contract for Migen, the transfer agreement between Brann and Skënderbeu (signed by Bekim as proxy), and only one final document remained before all the paperwork was completed: the International Transfer Certificate, or ITC. It's a standard form where the selling club should list chronologically which clubs the player have played for, how long, and if the player's childhood club should receive education compensation or solidarity funds. It's an intricate system of compensations in order to give something back to the clubs where the player started, should one of their players become a professional. There is a lot of tricking going on with these compensations, as could be seen, for instance, with several of John Carew's transfers, where Lørenskog ended up on the losing side. In 2013, eight full years after Carew was sold from the Turkish club Besiktas to Lyon in France, after numerous requests to FIFA both with and without lawyer, Lørenskog received the solidarity funds they were entitled to – around 200 000 euros. In principle, the selling club shouldn't sign the ITC until all money transfers are completed, including the transfer sum between the clubs.

In many international transfers, especially from Eastern Europe, not to mention Africa, it can be a great challenge to get hold of a signed ITC. A transfer I did later to Molde – a Ghanaian left back – was problematic. In this case, the player's club had signed the ITC and sent it to the Ghanaian Players' Association, all according to the rules. All associations should oversee which players are transferred into and out from their country. The procedure in this case is that the Ghanaian association enters the transfer in their archives, and then send the ITC directly to, in this case, the Football Association of Norway. However, the association in Ghana refused to forward the document. A bribe of 15,000 U.S. dollars was needed before they finally let go of it.

In other words, this document is a vulnerable part in international transfers.

In theory, this should not be a problem in Migen's case, since Bekim had a document authorizing him to act as proxy on behalf of Skënderbeu. In the authorization given to Bekim there was also listed an account number to Raffaissen Bank in Albania, where

Brann should deposit the agreed transfer amount of 100,000 euros.

Brann did everything according to the regulations, transferred said amount and entered it into their accounting system as the buying club according to the correct procedures defined by the local authorities.

The only thing lacking now was the ITC, which Bekim should fetch in Albania. He went there in the same instant the money left Brann's account, and they arrived more or less at the same time in Tirana, twelve hours later.

What Brann and I did not know, was that the authorization document from Skënderbeu was as fake as a three-pound coin. Moreover, the account number was for one of Bekim's own personal accounts. He'd had his own scheme all along.

Bekim got into the car, and drove (like a pig I assume) the six hours to the world capital of sheep's brain soup – Korça.

There he met with the owner and president of the football club Skënderbeu, Spiro Bardhi.

What turned out to be the case, in stark contrast with the information Brann and I had received, was that Bardhi had approved neither Memelli's trip to try-out in La Manga nor authorization for him to sign a contract with Brann.

He was furious.

As mentioned, Bekim has a sinister side to his personality. I know more about what happened that night than I care to tell. However, the result was that the ITC was "signed" by Spiro Bardhi, and the next day the final document for completing the transfer was sent from Albania's Football Association to the Football Association of Norway NFF on Ullevaal.

A journalist from the local newspaper *BA (aka Bergensavisen)* had managed to get hold of Bardhi's mobile number and, ever the thorough journalist, wanted to get a statement from Migen's previous club about which type of player the Brann fans could expect to see the next season. Normally a feel-good interview of the type that often gets ample coverage in the dead time between seasons, when the sports reporters are struggling to fill their daily quota.

The next day, the major headline on the front page of BA was:

BRANN ARE THIEVES!

A furious Bardhi had told the reporter that he had been duped, and that Migen could expect a 3000-euro fine for trying out for another club without permission. And finally, that Brann in no way should think that this matter was concluded as far as Skënderbeu was concerned. This would have consequences!

Bekim, still in Albania, got into his car and took another, probably hazardous, drive to Korça to pay the club president Spiro Bardhi another visit. After some old school Balkan persuasion, Bekim made sure that there were no more complaining from that side, that the International Transfer Certificate was signed again, this time with the real signature, and everything was sorted out for real. As mentioned, Bekim had his sides, but he was also my tutor when I was a novice in the football agent business, and that's something I will always be grateful for.

AGENT WITHOUT A LICENSE

Failing the agent exam in March 2006 was a major bump in my road to becoming a full time agent. With the transfers to Rosenborg BK and SK Brann, my business was getting started. My network was growing, and I worked hard towards the oncoming summer window. Having considered the exam a formality, I was annoyed at myself for a long time for not taking it seriously enough. I had told all the clubs, players and other agents that my license was just around the corner. After all, I couldn't take the test until March – no one could. And that explanation was good enough everywhere. Jostein Flo was among those who thought I had a license when I visited him a few days after the failed exam.

I was sitting in Jostein's sofa in his home in Røyken, southwest of Oslo. It was late Wednesday morning at the time of year when the series was about to start in 2006. Jostein was almost my neighbour at that time – only a three-minute drive from my house in Spikkestad. Nevertheless, this was my first time at his place. We had only spoken a few times on the phone during the weeks before. We were watching a DVD with clips of a player on the national team of Macedonia who I represented in Norway. I was nervous as hell on my way over to him, since the business of selling football players was a pretty new and unchartered territory for me. But there was no reason to be nervous. Jostein turned out to be an even more relaxed and laid-back person even than the relaxed and laidback impression he gave on TV. After several cups of coffee with the DVD on, chatting just as much about ladies as about football, I felt almost like his buddy.

The oldest of the Flo brothers is definitely a straight guy. Cave man type. His house has an open living room design, with no door out to the hall where there is a small lavatory. There I sat, relaxed with my hand hanging over the sofa, half turned in the direction of the lavatory. All the coffee had had its effect on the Strømsgodset director's guts. So now he was sitting on the loo with his pants on his knees, door wide open, talking to me.

– *I like the player, Knut. But what's the economy in this?*

He asked, before I heard:

– *Hnnnng, phew. That was a tough motherfucker! My missus is experimenting with all kinds of nasty healthy food in the kitchen. Kills my ass.*

When I had decided on a career as football agent, I had imagined that one of the toughest challenges would be to get a foot inside the clubs, build networks and get in touch with the people making the decisions. I had imagined several scenarios, and as a main theme expected lots of rejections and in best case short meetings with uninterested club leaders. However, not even *my* sick imagination had come up with a scenario where I was negotiating salary and transfer fee for a player, with a Director of Football while he was taking a dump with the door open.

He finished and flushed. But neither of us blushed. We chatted a bit more, and agreed that I should send him a mail with the economic details. We shook hands, and I was back in the car. Taking a shit in front of a new contact was definitely an icebreaker. Or more like an ice smasher. I felt like an old friend of this tall guy from Stryn in Western Norway.

After the small mental downer of failing the exam, I decided to push on in the same pace towards the same goal. I had many balls in the air, and if I could land only one or two of them during the summer, the fees would probably be enough to build a solid foundation for my agent business. After all, Jack Karadas had worked for a long time without license, so I should be able to do the same. As long as my intentions were good. And they were. The week after I failed, I sent a letter to the association telling them I was planning to retake the exam in September.

I mostly kept the truth about the exam to myself, by not telling any business associates about my failing. The few times someone asked me directly if I had the license, I lied like a drunk sailor. I made up stories about insurances that needed more time to be sorted out, papers being sent here and there in various systems. I basically said what occurred to me at that moment, and after a while, it had boiled down to a more or less credible story. But I also noticed, to my great surprise, that the clubs, and especially those who really wanted one of the players I was representing, didn't care too much about whether I had a license or not. I got the impression that formalities and regulations were more guidelines than strict requirements, and that there was a secret way around most obstacles.

When the opening of the summer window was ending, I had already completed several try-outs with players in various Norwegian clubs. I didn't have any contract offers yet, but I was proud of myself for what I had accomplished in such a short time. Not only economically, but also the network I had built. I was on familiar terms with many people who I had admired but only known through the media less than a year ago. At the same time, the admiration I used to have for these people was rapidly declining. When I actually met, shook hands and talked with my idols – players, directors of football or club leaders – I already had a comprehensive impression of them from newspapers, TV, radio and the web. The media presents them as great athletes, in the middle of their career or with an impressive career behind them, people who know what they are doing when it comes to tactics, training methods and especially player logistics. The average person gets the impression that all new player acquisitions are thoroughly assessed over time, discussed back and forth internally in the club between the coach team and the athletics management. And that all this funnels out as a sum of professional knowhow and experience that results in signing a new player. Nothing could be further from the truth.

Even when clubs make unsuccessful acquisitions over and over again, they always seem to have a bunch of reasonable explanations when facing "the court of the media" after throwing away millions. The media buys it, so we buy it too. The truth is that surprisingly many player transfers are based on little and/or inaccurate information and quick decisions with few people involved. There can of course be large variations from one club to another, and from one director of football to another. Some transfers do happen in a way that is pretty close to the impression created by the media, while others constantly make fast decisions based on info from a single source – who often turn out to be both a buddy of the Director of Football and a casual agent for the player in question. When a director of football or coach switch clubs, a pack of agents from his inner circle follows him. The result is that as an agent, you can suddenly lose access to one club, while a new door opens a completely different place. This has happened to me several times. It's a known fact in the business that if an established coach/agent team suddenly comes into a club where you have earlier had good access; you are out in the cold in a snap. In other words, the quality of the players a club purchases depends heavily on the network to which the club's coaches and athletics team have access.

In 2006, I was in the middle of a hectic phase of network building, and one of the year's highlights in that respect was the World Cup in Germany in June. Through my colourful and slightly crazy partner, Bekim, I got to know a German-Bosnian guy who lived in Hamburg. His name was Vladimir, but I called him Vlado. Vlado looked like a stereotypical white collar mafioso. He treated me like a king, and we had a great chemistry. We spent the days in Hamburg in a luxury hotel in St. Pauli, close to a park area that was closed off and reserved for supporters from the various countries. Each night we got together in an Italian restaurant in a fashionable residential district; a scene that could have been taken straight out of the Godfather movies.

The restaurant was at the end of a street, with a small park outside. It had few tables and an exclusive, but cosy atmosphere. Its owner, Roberto, looked just like the puppet master Geppetto who pulls Pinocchio's strings – an elderly, not very tall, gentleman with a full moustache and a grey mane of hair that moved in rhythm with the typical Italian gesticulation that accompanied his talking. A lovely, warm handshake and grandfatherly smile. Everything about the place was comforting, and one Italian dish after another landed on our table, served by discretely dressed and stunningly beautiful Italian ladies. They never spoke, just smiled timidly each time you thanked them for another refill of Brunello in your glass. The talk flowed easily around the table every night, and people came and went. They were all men, and everyone greeted Geppetto respectfully. One night I ended up signing a cooperation agreement between Vlado, myself and a strange guy from Israel. He was a medical doctor, running a ward at a hospital in Tel Aviv, but in reality, he mainly worked as a football agent.

Without a license of course. He was involved in more or less all players moving into and out of Israel at that time.

To make it simple, I am just going to call him the Doctor. The deal included specific details about our common responsibility, what each of us was obliged to do, how the fees should be distributed for given situations, and finally that each of us should put up 10,000 euros as a token that we took the cooperation seriously. We agreed that Vlado should hold the combined 30,000 euros.

I was very impressed by Vlado's network, and my impression peaked one night after we had watched Argentina beat Ivory Coast 2–1 from a VIP lounge on the AOL Arena (now Imtech Arena) in front of 50,000 cheering spectators. It was an even and very well played match, and one of my favourite players in the world, the mega star Didier Drogba, scored the only goal for the Ivory Coast.

During the conversations at Roberto's restaurant later that night, I mentioned Drogba several times, why I liked him better than other stars and which of his qualities I valued. At that time, he was considered one of the world's top football players, and everyone wanted him, all the time. Wherever he went, he was protected against media and fans. After a while, and a few glasses into yet another delicious Brunello, Vlado suddenly asked me:

— *Knut, since you like the guy so much, would you like to meet him?*

— *Meet who, Vlado?*

— *Drogba, of course. You have been talking about him all day, why not tell him how you feel to his face?*

I laughed heartily and told him that of course I would like to meet him.

— *What if he could just pop into the restaurant with us?* I asked, and laughed some more.

— *Why not?* Vlado said. And picked up his phone.

After a while, someone answered at the other end. The others at our table – guys who obviously were very wealthy with no apparent nine to five job – kept on talking about other things. They were not visibly impressed by Vlado's suggestion. I, on the other hand, was stunned.

Vlado spoke calmly in German and had a stern and concentrated expression when listening to the phone. The conversation became more and more energetic. At a point Vlado raised his voice yet another gear, and now I could clearly hear the guy he was talking to screaming in the other end. Vlado switched to Bosnian. He got up. Walked around in the room as if he was the only one there, while screaming at max volume. The other restaurant guests lowered their heads and turned their gaze from him. I got the impression they had witnessed this before, and knew the proper conduct in these situations. Roberto, who until now had been in his customary spot behind the bar, humming along to the gentle Italian background music, stopped his humming. He calmly put down the large red wine glass he had been polishing with a cloth, and threw the cloth gracefully into a sink. He approached Vlado with short steps, stretching out his hand against him as if he was preparing to grab something. Vlado saw him coming, said two short words into his mobile before handing it over to Roberto. The little man addressed the guy in the other end politely, and spoke with a calm, warm voice. A few sentences were exchanged, before Roberto said ciao and hung up.

He handed Vlado his phone back, and said:

– *Didier will be here in twenty minutes. I'll make you something tasty.*

Then he went back to the bar, humming on as usual.

Not only did Roberto look like Geppetto from my childhood memories. He also knew how to pull some strings.

Didier arrived, and I was star struck. It would be the mother of all exaggerations to say that he felt the same about meeting me. Long story short, he found himself on the opposite end of the enthusiasm scale. However, he was a decent guy, and put on his best smile. That's how he ended up in the restaurant with us, for twenty, for him probably the most boring minutes of the World Cup that year. Let us just say that I'm pretty sure the memory of this event is clearer to me than it is to him today.

My life without any agent's license had so far turned out far better than I had feared. The new cooperation with the Doctor bore fruits – there were many opportunities. However, it was an e-mail from Øystein Neerland, at that time Director of Football in Molde Fotballklubb, that brought up my most smarmy fox grin.

SUMMER TOUR

Could it really be? I thought. Molde too?! Do they really pay up almost a million euros for a player, based solely on a thirty seconds YouTube clip? I pinched my arm. I needed to act quickly, to strike the deal while the iron was still glowing red-hot.

It all started with my reading in an online newspaper that Molde needed a new forward. And the Doctor, my newly found Israeli friend, had the cure. He was in contact with a South-American forward who played on the national team of his country. In the e-mail from the doctor, he had included a link to a YouTube clip, where you could see the player scoring four goals in a cup final. The quality of the clip was rotten, and it only lasted 30 seconds. Nevertheless, four goals are four goals, and there were many spectators at the match. He looked good.

I searched the web and found the name and number to Molde's Director of Football, Øystein Neerland. In the phone, I introduced myself as a licensed agent offering him an exciting player. Neerland seemed positive and told me to mail him. Which I did, including the link to the aforementioned YouTube clip. The next day he replied and told me they were very interested, and wanted to know more about the economic terms. That was the start of a memorable trip to the jazz capital of Norway.

The forward's name was Dante Lopez, from Paraguay. He was 22 years old and played his first match for Paraguay's national A-team two years earlier. Now he was playing for the Paraguayan top team Club Olimpia, and had put up an impressive 12 goals in 18 matches in the series, plus the 4 in the cup final that was documented in the shitty, but valuable, YouTube clip.

With stories circulating that Lopez was close to signing with a Serie A club, but that there were problems getting the permission to play in Italy, the negotiations proceeded in record speed. After only a few days of phones and e-mails between South-America, Molde Fotballklubb and myself, we agreed on a transfer amount of 900,000 euros and a salary limit of 250,000 euros per year in a three-year contract. It's common in South-America that several investors have ownership interests in a player, in addition to the agent; and that was the case for Lopez as well. Both Molde and I scented that many people on the other side of the Atlantic wanted a slice of the transfer cake, so Molde instructed me explicitly that they didn't want any trouble when we came to town. Max one representative for the player was welcome in addition to me.

So far so good, and all that was left seemed to be a good celebration of yet another contract. So I invited a friend from Bergen along with me to Molde. I was to meet up with both him and the people from Paraguay in Oslo Airport, Gardermoen, and take the last flight to Molde the same night.

Therefore, I was *very* surprised when I spotted the celebrity forward and his company entering the arrival hall. Six men in suits plus Dante Lopez himself. A motley crew, and every one of them, including Lopez, topped my own usage of hair products with a solid margin. Moreover, there was a bad mood between them. What the hell was this?

The flight to Molde was almost empty except for our strange delegation. I took the opportunity to ask them to verify that there weren't any changes in the economic terms of 900k plus 250k euros. That triggered a quarrel between them, and I became spontaneously soaked with perspiration and felt sick to my stomach. The matter was already in the media, and the transfer was supposed to be a positive headline in the local newspaper *Romsdals Budstikke* the next morning.

I understood quickly that both the transfer amount and the salary was much lower than what they wanted, and that's why there were so many of them and the reason for their quarrelling. The mood was disastrous when we landed, and the representative for Molde wasn't impressed by my eager attempts to smooth things out. But in the end, he trusted me when I promised him that everything would be all right as planned the next morning on Aker Stadion, where medical tests and signing of contracts would take place.

Luckily Frank, my buddy, and I had booked at Rica Seilet Hotel, the city of Molde's humble copy of Burj Al Arab, while the circus company were to stay at Thon Hotel downtown. They went in their own car to their hotel, while we went in a taxi to ours. The driver was a cool dude with long hair and much love for his home team, Molde.

He had noticed that we were part of the player group in the scrum outside the airport, so we had a good chat during the drive into town and my spirits rose somewhat.

Frank went straight to the bar, while I went to the room to figure out a strategy for the next morning. After a few hours of hectic phone meetings with the wild bunch at the Thon hotel, including some necessary screaming and threats from my side, I felt reasonably safe that tomorrow would turn out more or less as planned. Well...

After little sleep and unnecessary amounts of alcohol, I presented myself newly showered and in my best suit in the reception at nine. Where I was met, as expected, with a full page in the local paper about today's big signing event at Aker Stadion. I don't know if it was the alcohol trying to get out of my system, but in any case, I felt sweat trickling down my spine. The sliding doors opened, and the entire troop entered. My suit got even hotter.

We didn't exchange a single word on the short walk over to the stadium, and my hopes that this was taken care of during the night, were dwindling. But there was no turning back now, and I envied Frank, who was snoring in his hotel bed now, in the seventh floor behind me.

We were welcomed by the director, Tarje Nordstrand Jacobsen, the chair and the coach, plus a medical team who brought Dante with them for a medical test right after we had been over the formalities. This was supposed to work smoothly – all the negotiations were completed in advance.

The meeting room was nicely prepared with cookies, fruit and coffee. However, neither sugar nor caffeine did much to lift the gloomy atmosphere, which was made even worse by the fact that there were only chairs for six people, which meant that half the delegation in suits had to stand along the wall.

My sweating started to become a real issue, and I ended up in a dilemma where I could either take off my jacket in an attempt to cool down a bit, or realize that that would make my soaked shirt very much visible for everyone present. I chose to button up my jacket in an attempt to keep the dampness confined. After all, if it came to the point where the perspiration was breaking through the suit jacket, I would probably already be on the losing side of the game. For now, everyone kept up appearances.

The director handed out copies of both transfer contracts and player contracts while informing us that all amounts we had agreed upon were already filled-in. We were encouraged to read it to verify that everything was in order.

It was quiet before the storm, and I had a strong feeling that all hell would break loose within a minute, with no other option than just observing it. You feel alive in moments like that. But you feel you are dying a bit too.

However, my worst assumptions turned out to be unfounded ... reality was much worse. What a row! As if by magic my Latino friends suddenly looked like a carnival troop who had just been told that their six months tour wasn't over the next day as promised after all – they had to take a two week's detour to Wetland Town first before they could go home to their family and friends. Dante's entourage were raging by the fact that Molde expected them to be ready to sign. They now wanted 1.3 million euros for the transfer, plus fifty percent of any resale. Moreover, Dante would certainly not sign for a salary that was anything less than 750,000 a year.

After a few seconds of genuine shock from the three Molde leaders' part, time caught up with us, and two of them got up in anger and told me and the clowns, in a display of dark northwestern fury, to go to hell. The coffee cups clattered when they slammed the door behind them. Director Nordstrand Jacobsen, being a diplomat at heart, remained seated – not saying a word, just staring up into the air. Even the boiling Latino blood chilled by the fury of the two Molde leaders, and one of the South-Americans seized the word.

Now they suddenly accepted the original 900,000 euros and 20% resale share. But, another one interrupted, they all had to get their flights to Molde covered. The director explained with diplomatic cold rage that he had been crystal clear about welcoming one representative only, and that they would only cover one plane ticket. The three Julio Iglesias lookalikes decided it was their turn to react like their colleagues from Molde had a few moments ago. More clattering of coffee cups. On the positive side, at least now there were seats for everyone.

I tried to take control, and reminded the remaining people that we were here to achieve a common goal. To make the negotiations even more absurd and less credible, Dante's agent now cut the salary demand in half, to 375,000 euros. For a short while it even looked like we might be able to find common ground somewhere around 300,000, but the director didn't yield a dime on this point. He even produced a summary of the salaries of all the players in the club, showing that with 250,000 a year Dante would be their best-paid player by a wide margin.

Nothing impressed Ali Baba and the three remaining thieves. Finally, the director lost his temper, got up and told us to screw this deal, even if Dante decided to accept the original offer. This was a final NO from Molde. He escorted us out from the stadium while calling the club physicians, who were now at the hospital taking blood samples. He told them that Dante could keep his blood and told them to send him back to his hotel.

We were standing outside the stadium like confused chicken in the summer breeze, and I felt my anger towards the Paraguayan General Stroessner supporters building up under my body fluid soaked suit.

But the gentlemen smiled cunningly and told me this was a good first round of the negotiations.

Surprised and confused I almost shouted:

— *What the hell do you mean by first round?! Do you really think this was a play from Molde's side? We're through, it's over, you can go home. Screw you!*

It was a style study of how six faces can change and twist into the strangest of expressions, and you could positively see the frenetic brainstorming going on behind their expensively moisturised faces. It looked a bit like a bad Monty Python sketch. Except that nobody laughed.

Reality dawned on them, and the fact that they hadn't grasped the seriousness of the situation earlier, made me if possible even angrier. From being a group of groomed businessmen with high confidence, they collectively transformed into young lads who weren't getting what they wanted. They became desperate, and told me after a short internal discussion in Spanish, that, yes, they were now willing to accept a 550,000 euros salary for Dante.

If I could please call the director to try to sort this out? I didn't have much to lose, so I picked up the phone, but to no avail. This had become a matter of principle for Molde, and they had closed and locked their door. A little later, the player himself arrived in taxi. He looked bewildered and enquiring. When I left them a few minutes later, the six lackeys were in a circle around a Dante Lopez who was frothing with fury.

Back in the seventh floor, I stepped out of my suit on my way into the bathroom. A cold shower was what I needed now, before I tipped a dizzy Frank over to his side of the bed. Time to get some sleep.

Around 5 p.m., Frank woke me up with a newly opened beer.

– *Time to celebrate, Knut, no more sleeping!*

He got a quick update, looked thoughtfully into the air, before a switch flipped inside his head, he handed me the beer again, and said:

– *Even better reason to drink then. Cheers mate!*

We were wasted, and we didn't leave the room until we had researched how long it took for various pieces of the furniture in the room to reach the shiny sea surface seven floors below. Four seconds turned out to be the average time. It was midweek, and only one dodgy watering hole was open downtown. Suited us perfectly.

The next time I woke up, I was in another room than the one I had swiped my Visa card to get. Over me was a home solarium, and beside me Frank's voice telling me we had to get out of there before the woman's husband got home from his night shift at seven o'clock.

It was cold and nasty in the fog outside the basement flat, but thanks to Frank, a taxi was on its way. Five long minutes later it appeared. We entered, and it made me strangely comfortable seeing the same longhaired driver with Molde in his heart sitting behind the wheel.

– *Well guys, this didn't turn out quite as planned. It's all over the front page of today's paper.*

He had room in his heart for us too.

We quickly packed our bags at the hotel while the long hair had a cigarette outside. I tried my best to avoid the front page of the local newspaper when we checked out. However, it was kind of like trying not to look at a woman's cleavage. The headline didn't make my morning any better.

The plane took off for Oslo, and I haven't set foot in the town of roses since then.

THE TOUR GOES NORTHWARDS

Tromsø needed a goalkeeper, and I had organized a try-out. Frank was still travelling with me – this was a short time after the Molde blunder. We should, as we had a few days earlier without much luck, meet the player on Oslo Airport, Gardermoen and take a flight together to Tromsø the same night. The candidate was a German-Bosnian living in Stuttgart. He had made a good impression on the phone, and it was a real joy to see him arriving all by himself, just as we had agreed.

Sead Ramovic, the goalkeeper, was a really funny guy, and we immediately hit it off. He stuttered as I had never heard before, but he had a great deal of self-irony, so even that became funny. On the flight to Tromsø, he showed me a DVD he had made himself for the try-out. Professional stuff, with TV recordings from the German Bundesliga, and he appeared to be great. My shoulders came down, and I was starting to look forward to the next day.

Director of Football Steinar Nilsen in Tromsø picked us up at Tromsø Airport, Langnes. He had reserved rooms at Rica, double for Frank and myself, single for Sead. I slept well that night.

Frank slept late, while Sead and I turned up at Alfheim Stadion at ten o'clock, as agreed. Sead went down into the dressing room to change, while the Director of Football and I found ourselves places on the empty stand to watch a training with eleven against eleven, directed to be able to witness Sead in a match setting. We waited for the players to enter the field, and I showed the Director of Football the DVD Sead had made. The clip started with a fabulous triple catch he did in a match for Wolfsburg against none less than Bayern München. Top notch. The director was silent, nodded a lot, and was obviously just as impressed as I was. The teams were ready, and the coaches signalled the start. After only a few seconds, there was an attack against Sead's goal, and his defender line backed quickly against their own penalty box.

"RAAAAAUUUUUSSSS!", Sead yelled. And again, *"RAAAAAUUUSS – Get out!"* I thought I heard him yelling a third time, but that was only the echo from the empty stands. All the 21 players froze, and it took several seconds before the game was going again. Awesome!

Nilsen, the Director of Football, got up and told me to accompany him to his office to look into the economy in this.

The fastest try-out in history was a fact. Only the negotiations remained. With Molde fresh in memory, I didn't order the Ferrari quite yet.

Initially I was happy to have Sead alone with me in the negotiations, but after a short while, I started to miss the six-headed troll from Paraguay. I know goalkeepers are known to be strong personalities and individualists. But that Sead should have at least six strong personalities inside of him, all stuttering almost at once, reconfirmed to me that I had made the right choice when I opted out of the psychiatrist education several years earlier. If some of the scholars got hold of this man, they could triumphantly write an entire new kind of diagnosis in the ICD-10 classification. Dead certain.

During eight intense hours, Sead managed to sign the contract no less than five times. Each time he signed, only minutes passed before he asked to get all three copies, mine, his and the club's, shredded them and then he asked for more money, car, apartment, less taxes, more plane tickets, shorter contract, longer contract, you name it. After he tore up the third original contract signed by all of us, I stopped putting them into the folder and down in the briefcase. It was easier to have them easily available on the table.

Around four I called Frank to tell him that this would probably draw out. He didn't object. He was sitting in a train wagon downtown, well into some beers, proclaiming that he could already confirm what he had heard about the blood in the Northern Norwegian female veins. It was boiling hot, and he was enjoying himself. Not that I had ever heard about any train going into

Tromsø, but I didn't feel like challenging that. Besides, I had other things on my mind.

The main framework of the contract we were trying to land, was a deal for the remainder of the year. In that way, Sead would be free to leave Tromsø and Alfheim without any compensation when the international transfer window opened in January. Besides a short term contract like this meant he would be eligible for artist tax, which is a fraction of normal taxes, more like a Biblical tithe.

As the agent, I was, just like the state, entitled to ten percent of Sead's gross salary, which Tromsø would pay me directly in addition to Sead's salary. Sead was offered 100,000 euros to play for the remainder of the year, in reality ten weeks. And with the mentioned tax rate, the corresponding hourly pay should be enough to make a living. However, money-loving Sead didn't want to pay his tithe. He wanted even less taxes. Therefore, he and the Director of Football started to work out a cunning scheme to circumvent tax rules and regulations, within the letters of the law of course – an art in which many directors of football have a black belt. They reached some sort of agreement where Sead's upfront salary was lower, while the rest of the money was paid via other means. In the end both of them smiled and thought this was a good solution. Contracts were signed for the sixth time, after a short pit stop to change the toner in the printer.

According to what had become standard procedure by now, we left the contracts on the table for the time being. At least that made them dry quicker and we avoided smudges. It's important to think positively. Minutes passed. Yet another cup of coffee was served, for I don't know which time that day. It was emptied, and the contracts still lay untouched on the table. I looked at the Director of Football, and the same thought went through our minds. I put my copy in a folder and down into my briefcase, while he went into his office to archive his there.

– *WAAAAIT*, Sead said.

We sighed. A booming laughter filled the empty restaurant at Alfheim stadium. It was personality number three, the hearty one.

– *Guys, you should have seen your faces. Relax, it's ok now. No more stress from me, I am satisfied.*

We shook hands, and it was a moment of real joy. As he opened the door for us out into the summer night, the Director of Football said casually:

47

– Knut, your fee is a percentage of his gross salary, remember? Have a nice evening.

I also remembered why I never play the lottery or buy raffle tickets. I never win.

On the other hand, bringing Frank along on the trip was a winning move. It's rare to have access to one hundred percent energy and positivity in human form. He is really worth his weight in gold. In addition, he had already arranged a double date with two lovely girls he met at the train station earlier that day. After dinner and a digestif, we met them as agreed at the bar in Tromsø's most popular nightclub.

I woke up the next morning because I was freezing. Before opening my eyes, I realized from the wind in the room that a window had to be open. It didn't help that I was only under a thin sheet – no duvet. Some speckles of blood on the sheet got me a bit worried. I quickly thought that I had probably fallen over during the night, or cut my hand or something. It's nice to lean on experience in situations like this, and I kept my calm. I went for a piss. In the corner outside the toilet, I found my duvet. It too had something that looked like bloodstains, and my pulse rose a bit. Then I noticed a bloody tampon stuck to the wall beside the window, and another similarly coloured fluffy thingy hanging on the window itself, and an explanation began to emerge. Someone had probably tried to throw them out the window. Women living together often end up with synchronized periods. Or so I've heard. I got the heat back in my body as soon as I remembered that the room was ordered in the name of the Director of Football. The stained bed covering wasn't something I particularly felt like explaining to him.

My phone rang. The display told me it was the very man I had in mind. He was furious. How could he know about the room? Had he been here tonight as well?

Nope. It was about Sead. He had dropped by the director's office before training that morning, to inform him that he had found a nice, roomy apartment in a central position for 1800 euros a month. He had already talked to the landlord, and it was no problem for him invoicing the rent directly to the club.

– Goddammit, Knut. We fucking agreed on this yesterday. Tromsø is not paying for his flat; he is paying it himself! You better fucking fix this or I am going to tear up the contracts this time. He hung up.

Sead was training, so I couldn't get hold of him for a couple of hours. Just as well. This agent wasn't ready to solve any world problems now anyway. For now, I just lay down on the stained sheet and put my arm over my face. Frank grunted, he saw what was going on, and cracked one of his tension-breaking one-liners that he really deserved to be famous for. It released burst of laughter that grew into a convulsive chuckling of the kind that usually only occurs the day after drinking, before all the alcohol has left your body.

Laughter and tears releases the tension in your body, and after a few gasps, life suddenly feels more worth living. A memory from a few hours back emerged, and turned out to be a way out. At least for a while.

This memory was of a charming man-eater I met in the lounge bar after the excellent dinner Frank and I had the night before. A bubbling happy, light-footed girl. Her name was Malin; she was from a suburb of Stockholm, and studying in Tromsø. In her early twenties, she dressed and acted just as I needed her to after some tiresome hours of negotiations. We talked a lot about her. Then some about me, and about Sead. I told her I wanted to find a place for him to live, not too expensive. Later that night, after a few more drinks, she said that Sead could rent the spare room she had, for 450 euros a month. It seemed perfect at the moment, as things often do when you are riding the happy wave of booze at night. Lying here the next morning, my gut feel told me otherwise. From experience, she wouldn't stand by her words in daylight. It had been the alcohol talking.

I was happy to discover that I had at least saved her in the contacts on my phone. It would have been a lot more difficult to find a Malin in Tromsø without her number. In retrospect, I would have wished it were more difficult, or rather impossible.

However, you only get hindsight in the future, so I called her immediately to find out. Sure, Sead could stay at her place. After all, it was only for a few months, and he was a football player so of course he had to be a nice guy. Intelligence and looks are connected, I thought. Happily, I called the Director of Football. I asked nicely if Tromsø could agree to pay 400 euros a month, and I would personally cover the remaining 50. After some wonderful Northern Norwegian swearing, we agreed. The only thing left now was to bring the good tidings to Sead.

He wasn't happy with this solution, of course, but after a reprimand even my old sergeant from the recruit school would have been proud of, he reluctantly agreed to try it for a couple of days.

We took a cab together to Malin's house that afternoon, and they immediately got along. It probably didn't make things worse that Sead is a handsome man that most women, and some men, wouldn't mind spending a romantic evening with.

The mood was good when I left them. I stopped by Rica to pick up Frank and our luggage. On the flight home, we had plenty to talk about – it had been eventful days for both of us.

I spent two days recovering from my visit to Tromsø. The Monday after I was still snoring until late with my phone on Silent. I was grateful for that when I woke up. No less than seven missed calls from Sead was blinking, and twelve from Malin. They had made their first attempts to get to me two minutes apart around five that morning.

To say that I felt sick to my stomach is an understatement, but at the same time, I felt a great relief for the 2000 kilometres between us. The safety of the distance disappeared abruptly when I got Malin on the phone.

– *What happened?* I tried.

– *I kicked him out, he cannot stay here*, she replied.

– *Tell me*, my heart sinking.

– *He came into my room tonight; that scum even sneaked into my bed!*

– *What are you saying, Malin!?*

The man who would become the best-paid goalkeeper in the history of Norwegian football, started both his professional and his personal career in Tromsø with a bang.

AND BACK AGAIN TO TROMSØ

After waking up from a dream and into a nightmare with the phone call from Malin, my only option was to take the bull by the horns, and the next available flight to the "Paris of the north". So I did.

About the only thing I knew when I landed at Tromsø airport, Langnes, was that things were pretty bad up there. And they were. Sead was out in a café, and Malin had packed his things back at her house. I chose to go and see Sead first.

As already mentioned, Sead has a humour and charm that can make you smile in almost any situation. He doesn't give a damn about his stuttering, and uses the time it takes to say what he needs to say. Today, many years later, we are still friends.

On this otherwise beautiful summer day in Tromsø, the man with the stutter was a stranger. A German with Bosnian heritage. I had the sole responsibility for bringing him to Tromsø, and I had begged Malin to rent him a room.

A man who now had abused my trust and stepped way over Malin's limits. I felt pangs of guilt. Walking down the street of Storgata towards the café, I felt a violent rage growing inside. As I entered, I saw Sead getting up, smiling. I was not charmed, and I entered filled to the brim with black rage. Yelling.

A lot of pressure had built up inside, and I had opened the valve. Sead tried to reply, but the stuttering made it difficult for him to give any sensible answers. To the other guests at the café the scene must have seemed absurd, and probably more than a little frightening too.

The dialog went more or less as follows:

– *What the FUCK have you done, you fucking stupid Bosnian idiot!!?* I yelled.

– *I am so goddamn angry I wanna kill you!*

– *But K-k-k-k-k-knut. I-I-I-I ha …*

– *Shut the fuck up. You are finished as football player!*

For people from the Balkans, yelling and gesticulation is a part of everyday life. Something that to a North-European may seem like a quarrel with a possibly fatal outcome, can in reality be an argument over which is the better lager. On any café in Bosnia, Albania or Serbia, my yelling at and shoving of Sead would look like any normal discussion among friends.

At the café in Storgata in Tromsø, in the middle of the day, this was far from a chat between friends. It was a scary experience for those around us. Sead, however, didn't react as much as I would have liked him to, which was rather to be expected given his background. Not until he saw the reactions in the faces of the other guests around us. That made his eyes widen, and he stopped his futile attempts to interrupt me. Just waited until I had finished my yelling.

When I finally shut my mouth, I was physically exhausted and had to sit down. We were both quiet for several minutes, alternately looking down at the table and meeting the other's gaze. When you are emotionally raw to the bone inside, you can communicate with looks alone. A lot.

The bartender finally broke our trance. He asked if we could please leave the premises. He was neither polite nor angry, just matter-of-fact. And very clear.

We left the café, walked through all of Storgata and on down to the quay, the fishing boats and the gulls. A cooling breeze together with a rank smell of fish sharpened my senses and cleared my thoughts. We sat down on a large boulder. Sead looked genuinely sad.

– *Sead, what the fuck happened? Tell me everything, from the beginning. And it would be best if you stick to the truth.*

I said it with a calm voice, feeling calm for the first time since I thanked the taxi driver for the trip that had taken me the last leg from the airport to my Gehenna for that day.

– *Knut, Malin is totally crazy. She is t-t-t-totally crazy, Knut!!*

I let him talk without interrupting him or helping him finishing his sentences. I still have the bad habit of finishing Sead's sentences when he stutters himself into a corner. Although I have heard that that's exactly what anyone with a stutter hates the most, I cannot help it.

On the quay in Tromsø, I bit my tongue and kept my mouth shut. Listened.

Sead told me he had moved into Malin's house with his things the same day I left Tromsø. Malin occupied the first floor of a horizontally split duplex, with living room, bathroom, kitchen and a bedroom on a small attic storey. Beside the bathroom, there was a door into a large room with a small, open kitchen and room for a bed, sofa and a small table. This was where Sead was to live, and in theory, they didn't need to interact except when they accidently ran into each other in the hallway, or both wanted to use the bathroom at the same time in the morning.

According to Sead they had a nice first evening together. After eating spaghetti he made and chatting a bit, they separated and went to bed. Around 2-3 a.m., Malin came in, woke up Sead and lay down next to him. And then some. Being a Balkan macho man, Sead had made in clear after the act that this didn't mean that they were together in any way, if that was on her mind. He wanted to be a bachelor. After which Malin left for her own bedroom, a bit offended.

The next day Sead went out at night with some of his new teammates, and brought a young lady back to his studio. Where they kept on until the young lady left the scene. Immediately after she closed the door behind her, Malin came trampling in to Sead.

She didn't want to house a man who dragged in any Moll, Nell or Sue from the street for an hour of love. They yelled and argued for a while, and finally Sead didn't see any other solution but to pack a small bag and leave. 30 seconds later both Sead and Malin opened the contacts on their phones and found *Knut from Bergen* and *Norwegian agent Knut*. But he was sound asleep.

Sead had finished his story. He looked inquiring at me, opened his arms slightly and shrugged:

— *So y-y-you see, Knut? I-I-I didn't do any harm. She is crazy; I'm telling you!*

I didn't reply, but looked at the fishing boat that had just come alongside the quay. Fishing is my second great passion in life, besides football. I would have given anything right now to change places with the carefree guy in orange rainwear, cleaning fish with a cigarette in the corner of his mouth and gulls all around him.

I am not a police detective, and I'm not even very good at telling when people are lying (pretty bad actually), but I memorized everything Sead said as best I could, and prepared for what I had dreaded most on the long flight up here. Meeting Malin.

– *Ok, Sead. Fair enough. You have had your say. Now go and book us a room on Rica. In fact, you can fucking book us a suite on Radisson Blu! And you're paying, for being such a jerk!*

I hadn't heard anything from the Director of Football nor from Rica after the episode with the blood stained sheets, but my gut told me this might not be one of my lucky days, so I didn't feel like challenging fate. A suite at the Radisson was a lovely thought. They have long, completely sun proof curtains, as if they were made of lead. I looked forward to that moment – hopefully not too many hours from now – when I could shut the world out with the led curtains. When the minibar and I could have a good time in hiding from the rest of the world.

But I still had some row to hoe before that could happen.

It was a half hour's walk to Malin's house. I wished it had been longer. Anyhow, the walk made me feel better, I had time to organize my thoughts and lower my shoulders a little, before I reached the gate into her garden. Malin stared at me from her large living room window. She was stunningly beautiful, a classical Swedish blonde, but with a completely blank expression. Empty eyes. My shoulders went back up to where they had started out during the few metres up to her entrance door.

I didn't need to ring the doorbell. She opened the door as soon as I put my foot on the last step. She stood wide-legged in the door opening with the same indefinable expression in her face.

The last time we separated, there had been laughter, high fives and warm, friendly hugs. The way I see it, the prevailing custom is that if you have started to hug someone, you hug every time you meet that person. There was definitely no hugs in the air this time.

She moved a little and said, almost reluctantly, *"Come in."*

On my walk over here, I had decided that I should definitely not start by giving her Sead's version of what had happened. Better let her play her cards first, so I decided to wait and see.

Apparently, she wasn't planning to start talking any time soon.

So I started with phrases like *How are you doing? This sucks, Malin! I am so sorry, what can I do?* etc. Her responses were mainly uninterested nods and snorts.

"Forget it", she repeated. *"The only thing I need from you, is that you take his stuff with you and get out of here. I am through with this."*

We continued the somewhat heated discussion, and I was more and more puzzled by her attitude. I wondered if this might be a typical reaction after an experience like this, and felt inadequate. Someone who knew more about the human psyche should have been here in my place.

She didn't budge, and showed no interest in discussing the matter. I played my last card, and told her Sead's point of view. When I came to the point about the young groupie, she exploded. She didn't even comment on his allegations that she had come into his bedroom at night and offered herself to him. She just yelled more or less the same to me as she had to Sead, in an unholy mix of Swedish and Northern Norwegian dialect that sounded like

– *Hell he cain't come dragging little girls in here at neight waking up the entire house with their facking!*

She told me to get the hell out, which I did. Two suitcases and a PlayStation 3 was his luggage. It was a relief to see the taxi arriving after a short wait.

Ten minutes later, I was lying starfish style in the bed in the hotel suite. I had just met Sead in the door on his way out to afternoon training. Sweet! Phone off, TV on. A lot of room service was added to Sead's bill that night.

Short time thereafter, Sead played his debut match for Tromsø, away ground against Hamarkameratene. Eleven seconds into the match, he let in his first goal. He could hardly have started out worse. During the next four years, however, he was acknowledged as the best goalkeeper in Norway and gave the city of Tromsø an extra dash of colour.

HAPPY BIRTHDAY!

When you are an agent, it is important to have a friendly relationship with the sports reporters. They can contribute both good and evil when it comes to selling players, but mostly good. A sports reporter in an average sized newspaper normally has to deliver minimum two pages of text to the paper every day. Moreover, these pages should have a minimum of meaning and relevance. In the middle of the season there is lots of material to choose from, and harder for the agents to lobby in pieces about their players. In the football free periods, both summer and winter, the possibilities are much better. You learn which reporters you can trust, when there is an understanding that things are off the record, and which to stay clear of. It's a joint venture of sorts, where both parties depend upon the other. The game between reporters and clubs is particularly entertaining. One of the most well known secrets in this game can be illustrated with the following example from the newspaper Bergens Tidende:

CHELSEA TRACKING SOGNDAL'S GOALKEEPER
From what Bergens Tidende have learned, the current league champions in England want to get the Pole Piotr Leciejewski to London for one week's try-out in September.

— I don't wish to comment on that. Talk to my agent, the goalkeeper said politely yesterday night.

Agent Knut Høibraaten doesn't want to make any statements either, and refers us to the Sogndal management.

Manager Egil B. Mundal admitted last night that the Sogndal management has been made aware of Chelsea's interest from "the community around Piotr". However, he rejects that Chelsea has made any official request to Sogndal yet.

Suddenly this piece of news was copied by several other media; even some English newspapers.

Reporters have told me that in nine times out of ten in cases like this one, it is the person who refuses to comment on the story, who is the main source of it. Apparently, this is a common phenomenon in political journalism as well. I have used this system three times myself, and it works like a charm. In addition, in the above-mentioned example I can assure you that the agent who didn't want to make any statements about the Chelsea rumours, was the sole source of them. Moreover, these rumours didn't have a shred of truth in them. The world wants to be deceived.

One of my strangest experiences with a sports reporter was at Vålerenga's training field by Valle Hovin in 2006. It was summer, and I had two young Macedonians on try-out there. They were assumed to be the greatest talents in Macedonia, but they weren't super-good, and the try-out had come to happen as a sort of reparation for me after some foul play from Vålerenga a few months earlier, when I had a young Albanian left back, Renato Arapi, on try-out. More about that later.

This was relatively early in my agent career, and as a newbie, you either have to know someone, pay someone or be unpleasantly pushy to be able to arrange any try-out. I knew nobody in Vålerenga, but I had had some contact with Petter Myhre, at that time Kjetil Rekdal's assistant coach. Petter, as I would come to experience, is a very different person from his fellow coaches.

Different in so many ways, but most marked in the way he didn't take himself overly seriously, and he didn't care about getting media coverage. He was simply a very likeable guy, and also very accommodating when I, being a total amateur, contacted him to suggest a left back for Vålerenga after having read in the newspaper VG the same day that they were in desperate need of one. Petter's discomfort with the media would change dramatically a few years later, when he got a permanent employment as sports commentator for TV2. A scoop for the channel, in my opinion. Especially since Petter has a very good knowledge about football, something that cannot necessarily be said for all his colleagues.

In the try-out period, I went to Valle Hovin every day to follow the training. The last six months I had watched several training sessions with Norwegian and foreign top teams, and there were many similarities from one club's training to another's. That's why I was very puzzled about the way Vålerenga's training sessions were conducted. The young Macedonians were on a week's try-out, and each day was the same peculiar spectacle.

First all the players entered the field, some in groups, others strolling alone the few hundred yards from the dressing rooms to the playing field. When everyone had arrived, the warmup started, led by an assistant or one of the players. Petter Myhre was always first on the field, greeting and talking to all the boys. Kjetil Rekdal, their main coach, was nowhere to be seen.

After warmup, everyone gathered around Petter while he explained the day's session: whether they should drill the first team or do drills for passing, wing playing, transitions or whatever. Around this time, Rekdal usually came strolling in. If I hadn't recognized him, I could easily have mistaken him for one of the 10–15 Vålerenga supporters who usually followed the trainings from the sideline. Vålerenga is very generous and including with their supporters, and it's always a good atmosphere by the field at Valle Hovin, with a free speech policy if for instance a match the previous day didn't live up to expectations.

Rekdal still directed zero attention directed towards the field, but spent the time greeting supporters, old boys players or others, and reporters in particular. Not until Petter Myhre had started the main part of the training did Rekdal start to focus on the grass mat, although not on what I expected him to focus on: the team and the boys he was so handsomely paid to pour his football wisdom over.

Instead he called the goalkeeper's coach, if he was available, the guy responsible for the team's gear, and finally Arild Rønsen. Rønsen is listed with a number of roles for 'Enga': writer, manager for the club's own TV channel, motivator, supporter … you name it. What Rønsen actually did on Valle every day, which apparently he was paid for, is still a mystery to me, but he is a likeable guy, no doubt about that.

Rekdal and company picked up a ball and went to an available corner of the field, generally on the opposite side of where the actual training took place. There they played the game of PIG in the entire hour and a half the players were training.

The game consists of kicking the ball to each other, with a maximum of one touch on the ball and one to the ground. If you don't manage to receive the ball, or if you make a foul pass to one of the others, so the ball touches the ground more than once, you lose the round and get a letter. The first one to lose three rounds is the P-I-G.

Loud and at times fretful discussions followed, about who lost the rounds, based on whether it was a bad reception or a bad pass. Rekdal in particular had a tendency to insist on his point of view, and especially if the debate was between him and Rønsen. Rønsen usually submitted. He hadn't scored under pressure in Marseille; consequently, he couldn't match his opponent's authority.

It is often easier to get a more correct impression of the game from a distance. And the motley crew on the sideline, myself included, often chuckled over the main coach's competitive spirit.

They repeated this act every day, and it made me wonder what exactly the responsibilities of a main coach were. But the small group were obviously enjoying themselves, judging from the laughter and good-natured bullying between them. The losing PIG had to pose with his ass towards the others, and let them use it as target for power target-practice. Rekdal played PIG with his heart on the outside of his football shirt, and lost only once during the week. They never quit in the middle of a round, and at least once that week the quartet remained several minutes after all the players had left the field, to decide who would get his ass kicked.

I have never seen anything like it. Rekdal seemed completely daft. He gave the impression of a lousy coach, more interested in perfecting PIG than his team. Therefore, I wasn't too surprised when I read the players' statements in Dagbladet the day after he was sacked from his next coach job, in Aalesund FK, the 27th of November 2012: "We trained like a pee-wee team!" The players expressed their dissatisfaction with Rekdal's efforts on the training field, but added that Rekdal's assistant coach in the capital of the stingy inhabitants of Sunnmøre, Kent Bergersen, fortunately was very professional.

I still don't know who in reality trained Vålerenga that summer, but I learned early that the assistant coach shouldn't be sneered at; on the contrary, he often has a more important role than most people think.

One of the days I was watching the training, I started chatting with a reporter – a young girl from the sports section of VG. We were both new to this game, and there wasn't much to write about that day, except for the new faces on the field, and mine was one of them. She dutifully noted the players' biographical data, info about their standards as football players and what I expected from the try-out. She also wanted to know more about me and how I had established contact with the Balkan market. I told her I didn't mind telling her about myself, but that I didn't want the focus to be on my person in the paper.

This was a rule I tried to live by during my agent career: media focus on my players, not me. I have probably missed a lot of PR because of that. Other agents have been much more conscious about this and often appear in various media. Anyway, the next day an entire page of VG's sports section said that Knut Høibraaten was planning to start importing players from Albania, and according to the same Høibraaten, Norwegian clubs were fools for not importing players from Balkan rather than South-America and Africa. The article also included a photo, allegedly of me.

I didn't understand anything when I got an SMS that morning: *"Happy birthday, buddy! But you sure as hell don't look good for your age."* The explanation soon emerged. The article was in VG on my birthday, more precisely my 28th one, and the picture they claimed was of me, was one in their archives of my father when he was at least 55.

I called the young journalist, rather cross about her breach of my trust, giving her a scolding so she started to cry in the other end. She had told the desk in VG about her promise, and that they should only write about the players on try-out. The desk had promised her, she said, and she was just as surprised as I was. I calmed her down, and she suggested she could write a new story with the exact content I wanted. No matter what, as long as it was related to football. I liked the idea, but I didn't have anything I wanted on print at the moment, so we agreed to stay in touch. She kept her promise, and I had my first insight into how the symbiosis with reporters worked.

This would turn out to be very useful in the coming years.

Neither of the two Macedonians got a contract with Vålerenga. I didn't seem to have the right karma when it came to Vålerenga. I already had one failed attempt with Renato Arapi. He had been on try-out for them several months earlier, and made a good enough impression to attain a contract. Three years, 50,000 euros a year. He accepted. The next day the club withdrew their offer. Their first choice – the Danish left back Allan Jepsen from Aalborg – had also accepted, and they picked him instead.

A lot depends on chance, and one short moment, the decision of a single person, can change an entire career. Just ask Lars Bohinen. In 1993, he played for Lillestrøm. Lars' efforts and standard that season did not impress Ivar Hoff, Lillestrøm's coach at that time, so he placed him on the second team. Not great for him, considering that Bohinen played for the Swiss Young Boys only a few months earlier. No doubt, he was in a weak period. Except for one match that year, Bohinen simply didn't play well. The exception was a match between last year's league and cup champions, respectively, called the Wurth cup – a match between Rosenborg and Lillestrøm on Ullevaal stadium. RBK won both the league and the cup the year before, but Lillestrøm came second in the cup. In the Wurth match, Lillestrøm won 2–1 after goals by Bohinen and Thomas Berntsen. Lars played well, and among the audience was Norway's national team coach Egil Drillo Olsen. When Mini Jacobsen was injured ahead of the World Cup match between England and Norway the 2nd of June that year, Bohinen was the first name that came to Drillo's mind. Ivar Hoff had already instructed Lars to play a match against Åndalsnes for their second team, but that wasn't going to happen. At the twelfth hour, Lars entered the national team, and he scored a beautiful 2–0 goal in one of the greatest matches, and scalps, in the history of Norwegian football. After that, Lars went straight to England and played for Nottingham Forest, Blackburn Rovers and Derby County for a period of almost ten years. It shows that coincidences often play a major role in football.

It was the same Bohinen, now in the role of Director of Football for Vålerenga, who both gave and withdrew the offer to Arapi. Arapi, needless to say, was devastated. He continued his career in Denmark, and returned to the Albanian league after a while. Letting him go was probably a wise decision of Bohinen though. After all, as Director of Football, Bohinen has managed to win six medals with Stabæk and Vålerenga, so he must be doing something right. Today Bohinen is one of the rare species of a former top player with a successful career as coach. After a successful year in Asker, Sandefjord Fotball offered him a contract. The players there were obviously not prepared for a new coach with English training culture in his luggage. His training regime in the winter 2013/14 was so physically hard that half of them were incapacitated with various overuse injuries. I am excited to see the results when his lads get through boot camp and become real warriors.

At Valle Hovin in August 2006 there was another coach at the helm, with a philosophy that deviated somewhat from that of Bohinen. Two weeks after my birthday article in VG, Kjetil Rekdal resigned his coach position in Vålerenga with immediate effect.

He was probably fed up of playing P-I-G.

MY INTRODUCTION TO NORWEGIAN
MATCH-RIGGING

In May 2006, fourteen years after my youthful adventure in Albania, I stood on the same beach where my dad had his house in 1994. I was invited to meet someone who wanted to talk to me regarding my job as FIFA agent (still without license at this point, but that would turn out to not matter very much in this case). For the time being, I knew nothing about this man or what he wanted.

Due to the rapid development in Albania, there were now lots of bars and restaurants where earlier there had been nothing but bushes and shrubs. We had agreed to meet in the beach bar of the classical Eastern bloc relic Hotel Adriatica. This was where the political elite in the days of old got together for summer holidays. Today the place is run-down, but it didn't take much imagination to understand how magnificent it had been once.

At the beach bar, there was almost nobody at the tables, only a few scattered tourists. No sign of my blind date. A waiter intercepted me and asked discreetly if I was the Norwegian football agent. I confirmed, and he told me to follow him. We went out of the bar and down the wooden walkway, built so that the hotel guests could avoid scorching their paws on their way to the water. Halfway to the water the waiter tapped my shoulder and pointed along the beach.

A few hundred yards away I could faintly see a person sitting at a table, utterly out of place between two sand dunes. The table was set with a cloth, plates, glasses and everything. It was almost like walking into an absurd scene from Monty Python, so if John Cleese was the man at the table, that would explain a lot.

I started walking towards him, and by the time I had taken the third step, both my shoes were filled up with sand. The distance I had to cover gave me plenty of time to ponder upon the awkwardness you experience when you see someone too long before you are able to actually speak to them. If I were to look at the man during the entire walk, I would have to nod and smile to him over and over, as if repeatedly greeting him and ensuring that, yes, I have seen you, and I'm coming your way. So to avoid this, I turned my head deliberately from side to side, looking with mock wonder at the magnificent landscape on one side and the ocean on the other. I ended up smiling and nodding to the nature and myself as if communicating to the strange man what I was doing. Pooh! After a bit back and forth, taking in the scenery, images and memories from this beach started to trickle into my head.

For right on this very beach, nine years earlier, I had held lumps of wet and bloody red sand in my hands. The reason was an incident extremely few people on this planet know about. My own private D-day.

That day I lounged in a beach bar on the opposite side of the walkway from where I was now. Although it was more of a gambling den than a bar. The premises, approximately the same size as an ordinary bus, was furnished with electronic poker machines along the walls. The machines were a bit hard to understand, so I got the only other person in there to help me. That is, the only one, except for the bartender who was in the innermost part of the bus, behind his counter. My helper, who was leaning against and over me while I was sitting at a bar stool by one of the machines, had just helped me winning the jackpot of the day – the equivalent of 40 euros – when a car skidded to a stop just outside. A man got out of the back seat and entered with long strides, straight towards us. As he closed in, he pulled a hammer out of his waistband and swung it with great force straight into the head of my helper. Because he was leaning against me, the collar of my shirt was the first thing he grabbed on his way towards the floor, so I lost my balance too on the stool and followed him in the fall. The attacker hit him once more, again on his head, and I heard a crunching sound. I could only see the white in my jackpot friend's eyes as he lay beside me on the floor. Incredibly, he managed to get up, and struck out against his attacker, but missed completely. Two others came in, and together they dragged him out to the street. As a hypnotized spectator, I followed them. They hit his head against a brick wall. Nasty sounds and disgusting fluids. Before I knew it, I was in the middle of a hell of a brawl. It ended with two men bleeding on the ground with severe head injuries. I had no doubt that one of them was dead, but I wasn't sure about the other one. A new car skidded in by the sidewalk, and it only took a few seconds before both men were lifted into each of the cars, which then disappeared in a cloud of dust. I was alone. On the other side of the street, I saw a police officer staring at me. It was obvious that he had observed the entire incident. Demonstratively he turned his back at me and walked off in another direction. I was having a kind of out-of-body experience myself. I stumped over the street and down to the beach, kneeled and pushed my hands down into the sand. Scrubbed blood and other nastiness off my hands. Sniffed, and smelled that I had peed myself. Not wet my trousers a little, but really peed in them, like when you wake up four in the morning after a night of heavy beer drinking. As the saying goes, *Never bring a knife to a gunfight*. But my advice is, *Always bring Tena for Men to a hammer fight*.

What happened that day made a sharp border between my life before and my life after. Before that day, I didn't know that it's possible to play movies at the back of your own eyelids. Nine years later, I still have my own private, micro movie theatre with the inside of my eyelids as screen, spectators in my eye sockets. The movie being played sent constant reminders further back in my head. Now, after all this time, and many movie nights before I was able to sleep, I had gotten used to this bizarre phenomenon. The snippet from my D-day was on repeat, and if I had been able to burn it all on a DVD, it wouldn't last more than around 20 minutes. However, the projector in my head had a strong tendency to focus on the director's favourite scenes, and freeze the highlights.

Anyway, this had become like a faithful companion by now, and it gave me a strange sense of security each time the show started. Although on the most stressful days, it could be a bit too many of them.

As I was walking towards the stranger out in the dunes, who

had insisted on meeting me, my thoughts raced around in my head, and several times I caught myself looking down in the sand to locate the red spot. Maybe it was still there, buried under layer upon layer of sand.

Focus, Knut!

With a self-inflicted mental slap, I pulled myself out of the past and into the present. I stopped two meters from the man at the table.

It was definitely not John Cleese.

The mysterious man by the lonely table at the beach had an impressive amount of dark curls on his head. With sunglasses on a large nose, a cigarette hanging from the corner of his mouth, and black suit with a black shirt, he looked like a living parody. And when he started to speak with a squeaking mouse voice, the comedy was complete. My shoulders came down a little, and I started to get curious about what he wanted from me.

After a few introductory polite exchanges and a mediocre wannabe-fancy lunch, he took off his sunglasses and revealed a pair of icy blue eyes. Not of the beautiful kind, that you can get lost in (not that I have any habit of getting lost in men's eyes), but of the sinister kind, like the villain in a James Bond movie.

Now that he clearly was getting close to the subject of our meeting, there was no pretty wrapping around it. He said:

– *I arrange results in selected matches for a larger organization in Malaysia. I have long had a good Norwegian contact, who has done a good job, but for several reasons he is not active anymore, so I am looking for a replacement, and you were recommended to me. And it's urgent, since we have a thing with a match between Moss and Aalesund. Do you have good contacts in Moss Fotballklubb?*

The expressions Silent as an oyster, jaw dropping, eyes as big as plates and a drop in the pants all work perfectly well on their own. And together they describe this young football agent sitting across from the mystery man on the beach that day.

Without really processing everything, I replied quickly that I had good contacts in Moss, but I hadn't been involved in match-rigging before, and that I thought this was difficult to accomplish in Norway.

– *Ha-ha! Difficult? Didn't you hear what I just said? We have already had a man working for us in Norway for several years, and with very good results. He doesn't work for us anymore, and we need a new one. The job isn't very complicated. Everybody likes money. In addition, Norway is one of the countries where buying players is easy, especially in the divisions below the first one. Because the players there generally don't make more than 25–50,000 euros a year, and with your taxes that doesn't leave much in the pocket. When you offer a player like that 20,000 euros in cash, most will accept. And best of all, it's very hard to detect, both for the player's own team, the opponents and the government.*

It was a surreal experience listening to this Muammar al-Gaddafi parody and his intimate knowledge of Norwegian football, our First Division and our salaries and taxes. My brain was working on turbocharger, and a new, dark world started to unfold in my imagination.

– *Why is it hard to detect?* I asked hesitantly.

He lit another cigarette, leaned over the table, smiled faintly under his bulbous nose, and started:

– *It is all very simple. In this case, Moss has to lose against Aalesund with at least three goals. If it's 0-3, 1-4 or 2-5 doesn't matter, as long as they lose with three goals or more. Therefore, you only need to buy max four players, maybe even just three. If you get the goalie in, you only need him and a defender. As long as a small group of players behind are in, they can make sure they let in the necessary goals. The rest of their team will hopefully fight like lions trying to turn the match, and even score goals. In that case, our men just make sure they adjust the result so it ends up as desired.*

As I said, very simple, and we have done this many times in Norway without anyone suspecting anything so far. You are so damned naive and gullible up there. Just remember that people are people and money are money, all over the globe. We laugh at the Norwegian clubs that don't understand what is going on.

He emphasized his point with a burst of laughter, which brought about a smoker's couch that made fully developed COPD seem like a mild summer cold.

After some spasms, wiping of tears and some after-coughs, he was back again in forward leaning position:

– *You get a suitcase from me with 100,000 euros. When you get to Norway, it's up to you to figure out how many players you need to buy and how much you want to pay them. If you only buy two – a goalkeeper and a defender – and pay them 15,000 euros each, that leaves 70,000 for you. See? And if you're smart, you can make them accept even less. Norwegian players are cheap … and stupid!*

New round of COPD laughter.

Long story short, I managed to duck out of the situation, and we separated as if we had never met. I saw al-Gaddafi disappearing on the beach towards the hotel as his cowboy boots, which I hadn't noticed under the table, whirled up sand in the wind. On his way to a new meeting with a new potential partner. The Moss match was drawing closer, and he had a job to do.

I turned towards the ocean and took a deep breath. I had managed to outwit the James Bond villain, and now I was staring out over the ocean, hoping that Ursula Andress would emerge from the water. However, no Ursula, or Halle Berry for that matter, came sashaying towards me from the waves. So I closed my eyes and took another deep drag of ocean air, while the movie projector whirred behind my eyelids.

The match was the next week. Result: Moss vs. Aalesund 0-5. With my knowledge of this match, it was weird to read the local newspaper *Moss Avis* the next day. Moss' goalkeeper Erik Holtan despairing over the fact that all five goals should have been avoided. Holtan himself was elected as Moss' best player, and I thought to myself that the person in question that al-Gaddafi had managed to recruit, was greedy and had limited himself to buying off only a few players. Maybe Holtan had received the offer too, but he had obviously declined. Kudos, Erik!

Several years later, I mentioned my meeting on the beach to Geir Bakke, who was Moss' coach at that time. He replied dryly, and somewhat relieved:

– *That explains many things I didn't understand that day we lost by five bloody goals. Fucking wankers!*

LICENSED

I had worked almost a year now as agent without a license. For the most part the year had consisted of travel, travel and more travel. I had met an enormous number of people in the world of football in a relatively short period. No matter where I went, I had noticed one thing in particular. An agent who is *really* an agent, enjoys real respect. While there were an abundance of people who called themselves "agents", genuine, licensed agents were much rarer. That was a much-coveted title, and many people pretended to have it. FIFA had grown weary of this, and set up a link from the cartel's home page, fifa.com. The link is called *Players' agents list*. Now the matter was crystal clear. If your name isn't there, you are not a licensed agent, end of discussion.

Therefore, when the day came for my second attempt to take the agent exam, I was more motivated than ever. I was much better prepared than last time. My confidence was soaring when I arrived at the same premises on Ullevaal. This time there were more candidates – around twenty of them. I recognized only one face from the previous exam. The rest had probably realized their limitations and run off with their tails between their legs. I knew what was coming now; this game was familiar to me, so it was a delight to observe how the freshmen were standing around the same tables like frightened chicken. I could almost feel their unanimous awe when the tight Association Secretary welcomed me with a smile. Everything was set for a good day. I had even taken out the necessary agent insurance.

At that time, you had to go through a small hell to get it done. No insurance companies in Scandinavia would even consider offering an insurance like that. With all the demands FIFA was making, and with the frequent media publicity about six or seven digit demands between players and clubs – whether because of violated terms or untried legal subtleties – the insurance companies found it almost impossible to calculate the risk in this kind of insurance, not to mention the price of the policy. They wouldn't even touch it with a bargepole. After much searching in despair, Vlado came to my rescue. He had some connections, and after a few days, DHL was at my door with a brand new insurance from an Italian company. A comprehensive document with many pages and a golden seal over the company's signature on the last page, *Notarius Publicus.* Old style document. Probably the coolest document I have ever owned, if you can use that word about an insurance policy. I had already paid for the insurance – 2000 euros. All I needed to do was passing the exam.

A quarter to ten the secretary confirmed that all the candidates had arrived. She apologised that nevertheless we had to wait until ten before we could start. FIFA regulations. In addition, the actual test had just started to tick through the fax machine, so it might linger a few minutes over before everything was copied and ready. Didn't matter to me. I already felt like an agent after having lived like one for some time now. It was more like I was here to pick up something that was already rightfully mine. The coffee was free, and there were plenty of juicy Danish pastries for everyone. Only the one I recognized from last time and I touched them. The rest were dancing with their inner demons.

The only thing that had me a little on the edge was an important phone call I was expecting. I had lots of iron in the fire, and worked closely with Vlado. We had agreed that he should call me half past nine regarding a very important matter. It annoyed me that he was late. He knew I had the exam at ten, and this was a phone call I simply couldn't miss. I *had to* answer it.

The minutes passed. I became more and more restless, and my confidence dropped in sync with the seconds' merciless ticking. At one minute to ten, I had become the most stressed-out of everyone present. I was way ahead of the freshmen both when heart frequency and attacks of sweating was concerned. Fuck you, Vlado! Ten o'clock. The lady from my fantasy six months earlier came out from her office with a heap of papers. She was ready. In the same moment when she pointed at an open door saying *enter, please*, my phone rang. I was startled. It was Vlado. I hissed a hello, and he apologised. I explained my situation, that the others were already entering, and that I had max one minute at disposal, maybe less. Vlado was efficient, and passed on a damn important message to me as simple as possible. I had to take this down. The grace of God manifested itself in a promotional pen for *Hurtigruta Carglass* on the adjoining table, and together with a little brown napkin, it made it possible for me to scribble down the main points of the message. The third time the secretary asked me to enter, I understood from the tone of her voice that she really meant it. I hung up without saying goodbye, and ran towards the door where she was standing. Bowed apologetically like an Indian tea waiter on my way past her, and got an indifferent nod in reply. I found a place and sat down.

From last time, I knew that the five questions regarding Norwegian regulations should be simple. I wasn't worried about them. So all my efforts were focused on getting the answers right to as many of the international questions as possible. All my expectations were surpassed, and I had a really good feeling when I had finished the first ten international questions. There were five international questions left plus the five Norwegian questions. I skipped down to the Norwegian ones first. They were harder than last time, but they still felt easy after a year's experience as an agent. I surfed through the last five international ones as well, and allowed myself a bit of carelessness when I laid down my pen before the half hour had passed. My confidence maxed out, and I made a point of making it obvious to the other candidates that I had completed, kind of radiating *well well, guys, easy as pie, right?* What a bloody senseless and borderline nasty thing to do! The FIFA lady too noticed that I had finished, and I was allowed to hand in my answers and go back to the café area to wait. I called Vlado again, but he didn't answer. I assumed he was busy, and made some other calls before I read yesterday's paper.

The wait was over, and the secretary came out of her office to address the herd waiting in suspense. Again, I wanted the result verbally, and there was no need for her to whisper.

– *Knut Høibraaten, you have passed. In fact, you have only one single error. As far as I can remember, this is one of the very best exam results ever in*

Norway. Congratulations!

The year before I was the last one to get my result. This time she read my result first, so everyone could hear it. If every word in the dictionary had a picture underneath it, a snapshot of me at that point would fit perfectly under *gloat.*

Two others passed, the rest failed. I couldn't care less. The world was mine.

I accompanied the Association Secretary into her office. Eager to get everything sorted and my status official, I slammed my impressive Italian documents on the table with a big smile.

Everything went smoothly, and I could soon log in at fifa.com, scroll down the main page called *Players' agents list*, and kaboom! My name was there!

I could hardly wait to go travelling and meet up with collaborating partners again. Bask in respect and glory. Very Important Person. As the icing on the cake, the Football Association of Norway's (NFF) General Secretary at that time, Karen Espelund, came in person to present me with my license identification. It's made of black leather with the word *Agent* written on the outside, and it can be opened just like an FBI ID, with photo, name and signature of *The President of The Association.* She let me have a look at it before presenting it to me ceremoniously, accompanied by a warm handshake. I have hardly ever been prouder. At last, I was one of the big fish in the game. With the official license and the cartel watching my back. Untouchable.

I wanted English text on my business card, and the official title I was allowed to use was *Players' Agent – Licensed by the Norwegian Football Association.* I told the Association Secretary that licensed agents usually are referred to as *FIFA agents* internationally. Was it ok with her if I gave myself that title on my business card and in my e-mail signature? She made it very clear to me that that was definitely *not* ok. In fact, it was strictly prohibited, and it could lead to sanctions if I didn't respect that rule. I was never to mix FIFA's name with my work, period. I nodded reassuring, that I would of course play by the book, but the business cards were already ordered. And they didn't change during my career as agent. With a fresh agent's license in my pocket, I was about to return to Tromsø on an unforgettable trip.

A BOY'S DREAM COME TRUE

The occasion was a match between Brann and Tromsø (TIL). It was scheduled for a Sunday, but the day before was reserved for a match between the old boys' teams of the same clubs on Alfheim Stadion in Tromsø. Brann demanded revenge after an ignominious defeat ten years earlier. It was a well-organized event, with a common gala banquet on Friday.

Per-Ove Ludvigsen from Brann had arranged it for me to attend the gala banquet as a part of Brann's old boys' delegation.

It was an incredible séance, and the Brann boys stole the show. Two of them had a spontaneous stand-up performance that lasted thirty minutes. Everybody were laying over their tables laughing. The Tromsø boys were booed out when they left early. They wanted a good night's sleep before the match. The old boys from Bergen had other plans, and it became a long night.

After several up-to-take-a-leak-trips back and forth to the bathroom, I woke up the next day around noon. Considering that the match was set to start at three, and that I during the night had been given the job as *water boy* for the Brann team (water=beer in this case), it was time to get out of bed. I bought 24 beers, distributed them evenly in four plastic bags, and put a few bottles of water strategically on top of them to conceal the real contents.

An hour before the match was set to start, I met Per-Ove Ludvigsen on Alfheim stadium, where Tromsø's old boys already were changed and starting their warmup on the artificial grass field. In the away team's dressing room, most of the Brann guys hadn't changed yet and had their heads more or less under their arms. Collective hangover.

Old habits got them into their red shirts and shorts and on with half-hearted plyometric jumps and knee squats on their side of the field. I easily smuggled the plastic bags down to the away player's bench, which could be mistaken for a bus shelter. The rumour about the contents in the bags spread quickly, and the players came by the bench in a continuous flow to maintain their fluid balance before the match started. At the counting five minutes before kick-off, everybody was present except for one: Inge Ludvigsen. Nobody knew where he was, but the match started anyway. There were plenty of substitutes. Frithjof Wilborn started as striker, but with a much more boring hairstyle than at the last showdown ten years ago.

It quickly became obvious that taking an early night had been a good move. The northerners easily controlled the match between slow-moving, burping Brann boys. And it wasn't as if nobody noticed. There were a surprising number of spectators – hundreds of people, maybe even a thousand, had showed up to watch the match. Many of them were visiting Brann supporters, well hydrated, singing for their old boys. A good atmosphere.

However, old, morning-afterish bodies aren't very well suited for football. One after another of the middle-aged Brann players limped groaning towards the bench with tension injuries, cramps or other problems. It became apparent that we would soon be in shortage of substitutes. Where was Inge Ludvigsen, Per-Ove's brother? His phone went straight to the answering machine.

He arrived in the middle of the second half. We all heard him before we saw him. He was standing on the top of the seating section behind the players' benches, singing, with a half full bottle of Jägermeister in one hand, and conducting his own singing with the other. When the Brann fans realized his condition, their cheering became ecstatic. Inge walked triumphantly down the stairs between the rows of seating. The spectators' focus had shifted from the field to the clown. Per-Ove shook his head in dismay, moved under the roof in the bus shelter, and pulled his hat as far down over his ears as possible. Even several of the players had halted to watch the show.

Inge took his time on his way to the benches where we were sitting. He hugged fans and shared willingly of his bottle. When he reached the barrier at the bottom of the stairs, he didn't bother to open the knee-high door. Instead he grabbed it, swung himself elegantly over the barrier and landed ski-jumping style on the artificial grass with an exaggerated telemark skiing stance and his arms out to the sides. Deafening cheering from the audience.

– *Hi guys, I know I'm late. But I have already changed, check it out.*

He pulled off his woollen sweater, and had the red warrior suit ready underneath.

– *I just need a pair of football boots, and I'll play the rest. I ended up on an afterparty in Tromsdalen, and spent the night in a caravan. Good thing I put my suit on underneath yesterday.*

He managed to stand up, but only barely. By now, the bench was filled with injured players, and several of them had taken their boots off due to pain in their ankles or feet. Inge grabbed the nearest pair. They were a size smaller than his usual boots. But after an acrobatics and clown show in a John Cleese inspired silly walking style, greeted with roaring cheers from the Brann fans, he managed to force his feet into the leather.

About the time he had finished tying his laces, the next Brann player came limping to the bench, face twisted in pain. Everybody looked around for the next available substitute, but it soon became apparent that there wasn't any. Except for big brother Ludvigsen. Searching looks turned into incredulous ones: *No fucking way, this man is drunk.*

But Inge was ahead of them, waved to the referee that he was ready, and was signalled onto the field. Just before he crossed the white line, he noticed that he still had the Jägermeister in his hand. He turned around and tossed it to me. Then sprinted to his place, central mid-field for the occasion. It all happened too quickly for anyone to react.

The clock indicated 25 minutes left of the match. Tromsø had a 2-1 lead, which ought to have been much more. Inge ran around like crazy, tackling east and west. He quickly snatched the ball from a Tromsø player deep into Brann's half. Then he turned away two players, looked up, and kicked a fantastic forty-meter pass towards Frithjof Wilborn. The fans went ecstatic and he got a standing ovation from everyone, including the Tromsø supporters.

Throughout the match, I had been helping myself generously from the bags, and now I took a manly gulp of Jägermeister. This was great entertainment.

But as expected, Inge didn't last too long. After five minutes, he started to support himself on his hips and/or knees more and more. His arms were so limp that when he made the sign that he needed to be replaced, it looked more as if he was folding his hands in a prayer. As we know by now there weren't any substitutes left on the bench. The injured players tried to figure out if any of them could manage the last fifteen minutes. Nobody volunteered. Then it happened.

Kjetil Knutsen opened his beak, and said the words I will never forget:

– *Knut, borrow a shirt and shorts in a hurry, you have to play for Inge.*

All my life I had dreamt about this. In countless daydreams, I had visualized myself out there on the field with a Brann suit, cheering spectators all around. I scored spectacular goals; the fans loved me and hugged me as I ran towards them after yet another perfect score.

Now my dream was about to come true. Although it was the old boys' team, they were all heroes from my youth. The fact that I was pickled myself, and had just swallowed my third or fourth gulp of Jäger, wasn't ideal, but my adrenaline flowed and my heart rate was up in the high. I dressed in a hurry and started to look frantically for some boots. No one had my size, but the owner of the ones Inge was borrowing, ensured me that his would fit, size 45. Inge looked relieved when the substitution was signalled. He used his last strength to jog over to the bench. I was super-eager, and shouted to him on the field that I needed his boots. He got the message, kicked them off and threw them over to me. I stepped right into them without untying. If you have never put on a pair of football boots, I can tell you that that's a nearly impossible task. Nevertheless, high on adrenaline I still managed.

Fifteen magic minutes. I ran around like an idiot, arm raised, yelling *here, here* and *mine.* I didn't touch the ball much, but two minutes before the end TIL's Bjørn *Bummen* Johansen came running energetically along the left side towards Brann's foul line. I accelerated to max speed after him, and moments before he would have passed the ball to an unmarked Tromsø player in front of the goal, I tackled him like I was Nemanja Vidic. The tackling was clear as a bell, and Bjørn almost took a somersault before he landed behind the fault line, while I was left standing with the ball between my legs. Spontaneous mega-cheering from the Brann hordes as they rose and applauded.

I delivered the ball to the nearest Brann player, who drove it on forward, then turned and looked at the supporters cheering and applauding towards me. I was on the verge of tears.

The match ebbed, and not a moment too soon for me. I was worn out and panted like a whale. Pat on my shoulder and smiles from the other guys on the team. On our way out Bummen came over to me and said "Not bad, that tackling", winking at me. In the local newspaper the next day, they didn't mention my name. It only said "Inge Ludvigsen replaced by someone we don't know, and who wasn't particularly on terms with the ball today."

The real Brann boys, the A-team, arrived Saturday night. I had texted a bit with one of them and agreed that we should go out together after the match on Sunday. At 11 p.m. I met with a recently showered Brann player near the city's largest disco. As all successful football players with an athletic body and well-filled wallet, he was an incredible chick magnet. It's pure joy to go out on a bar with him, bask in his company and literally feed on the leftovers from him. After all, he can only have so many ladies surrounding him, and when they see that I'm his buddy, I am a good consolation prize. I am instantly promoted two divisions up in the ladies' league when I hang with him. Moreover, they pick *me* up, not the other way around.

Dazzled by the alcohol and all the lovely breasts surrounding me, I let the champagne flow. Money wasn't an issue that night. I gulped down one glass after another, and around two I was utterly pissed. An epic mistake in hindsight, since I with one hundred percent certainty could have enjoyed both one and two women at my hotel that night. However, when I get really drunk, I switch to auto pilot, and I have, as many others, an unique ability to navigate home regardless of my condition. I told my company I had to get to bed, and he nodded. As I was leaving, he grabbed my shoulder and whispered in my ear:

– Could I get the key to your room, and they'll give you a new one in the reception? The guy I live with gets really pissed off at me when I get back late, so in case I stay here till they close, I might come and sleep at your place. Ok?

– No problem, buddy. Here you go. And maybe I will see you later, or at least tomorrow. Good night.

One of the ladies accompanied me outside, delightfully eager. A little making out and petting by the 7-Eleven in Strandgata, but, alas, my manhood wasn't on my side, and I ended up literally retreating to the hotel with my tail between my legs.

Back in my room, after getting a new key in the reception, I stepped out of my clothes on my way from the door to the bed. I always sleep naked, it's the best way, and now I fell asleep before I hit the pillow.

Something jerked me out of my sleep. I opened my eyes. The heavy curtains kept the light out, so the room was pitch black. I lay naked on top of the cover in a slightly strange position, on my belly, halfway on my side, with my ass sticking disproportionally high up in the air. And on my ass I felt a hand cold as ice holding my left buttock. Pushing me slowly up and down. I was dead quiet, trying to listen. Some breathing and a faint moaning. The moaning came from a woman, I had enough practise to discern that much. I quickly realized that it was the Brann player who had brought a woman with him, and now they were lying beside me doing it, him on top. He was supporting himself against my buttock to get a better leverage. Smart. Skilled.

So what? No big deal, I thought. But do they know that I am awake? And if not, should I make them aware of it? Better not. They didn't seem to notice, now that I could see their outlines after my eyes had adjusted to the dark.

I lay like that a couple of minutes, and noticed to my mix of delight and astonishment that I was getting a little horny.

And *The Scoundrel*, as I call him, started to wake up there under my raised bottom. *Where the hell were you when I needed you at the 7-Eleven earlier?* I thought. However, before I had time for a deeper analysis of the issue, my attention switched to another physical necessity squeezing its way through to my conscious mind, among other places, with an abrupt force and determination. Before I had time to decide whether this was one of those that came with the option of sending it back into the intestines for later release or not, it went off with a bang. I have inherited farting from my father, and he is widely infamous for his *bangers*. This one would have made dad proud.

The two next to me froze in an awkward position in response to the blowout. Two long seconds passed.

The lady leaned up and kissed the Brann player hungrily on his mouth. He tightened his grip on my buttock, to the point where it

almost hurt, and they were back in rhythm.
It took some time before I was able to sleep.

SPOONING WITH BRANN'S DIRECTOR OF FOOTBALL

A recurring task during my first year as agent was assessing players, both new talents and more established ones. I wore my own "football glasses" and had my own opinions about who was good and who was not, just like hundred thousands of other football fans in Norway. And the average football supporter's ability to spot talent shouldn't be underestimated. You don't need to be a great player yourself to spot if another player has talent. Still, the business puts more weight on the opinions of their own people. As a retired junior player, I didn't have the same professional credibility with my clients, the clubs, as someone who has played on a high level for 15 years. *Some* professionals in the Norwegian football business do have unique skills in this area, but they are a lot more scarce than you would think, something that's evident from the many bad buys some clubs do under certain coaches and directors of football.

That is why I felt I needed a good and solid teammate, someone who could contribute athletic competence and expertise to my business. The greatest Brann warrior in my youth was the centre back Per-Ove Ludvigsen – already mentioned several times in this book in his later role as Director of Football in Brann. He was both an old hero and a competent football director. Naturally, I was delighted when he became my joint owner and colleague in my agent company in January 2007.

Ludvigsen is the closest thing to a Greek God for football fans from Bergen, after Roald "Kniksen" Jensen. In Fyllingen, the team from the district with the same name, where Ludvigsen was born and raised, he formed a centre-back duo together with his one-year-older brother, the party man, Inge. Together they were one of the main reasons for the district team's success in the early 90's. In 1993–94, Per-Ove Ludvigsen was at his peak, and very close to signing in Glasgow Rangers. However, a serious knee injury just before the contract was about to be signed in Scotland, set him back. He injured his knees early in his career when he played for Fyllingen. His club only had a half inch of bad artificial grass over a surface of flinty concrete on their home field. When Scotland was cancelled, Per-Ove went to Brann instead, and started a career there that would give him a legendary status in the city of the Seven Mountains. Per-Ove was a local alley cat many could identify with. He didn't feel the need to fix his hair before, during or after a match. He used direct language in interviews, and he wanted the focus on the team rather than himself. He was the captain, and he was our hero.

This thing about football players and hair is something I both hate and love. It's fascinating how well-paid men, on the most important working day of the week, just before a match is about to start, manage to focus on how their hair looks before going on the field. It's the last thing on their mind as they leave the dressing room! During the match, several of them have to fix their hair after heading or tackling. Take Thorstein Helstad, a king on Brann Stadion in his time. We loved him, and he was a fantastic scorer. Nevertheless, someone who is that obsessed with his hairstyle, having hair products costing the equivalent of a decent day's wage for the average supporter slapped onto his head before each match, never becomes a true war hero. It's difficult to identify with a player like that.

That is what made Per-Ove special. He could have been your neighbour, your dad, the mail carrier or the forklift truck driver on the quay. He was one of us. Moreover, Inge, his big brother, came to Brann the next year. That season, when the brothers played in the centre defence, was a high, because they played together, but also because of the way Per-Ove cared for his brother. Ludvigs, as I call Per-Ove, was a few good notches above his brother on the field. But while Ludvigs was relatively quiet outside the field, Inge was in a league of his own. He was frequently seen out on the town with something good in a bottle. He had tremendous highs and lows, both physically and in regard to his moods. The younger brother – the captain – often stepped up to defend his more complex half and watched out for big brother.

Per-Ove's knee was a recurring nightmare, and Brann tried everything – really everything – to try to fix the bugger once and for all. One season Per-Ove had to get an anaesthetic shot directly in his knee before each match. He was numb in his leg from his knee down, and he almost had to relearn how to walk – trust that his foot actually did what his brain told it to do, without knowing for sure whether his boot was positioned where he hoped it would be. In the most painful matches, he had to get a second shot in the break, and on one occasion he had to run to the sideline in the middle of a half to get a refill. But no one in the crowd or in their homes noticed anything in his play. It was like something taken from an American sports hero film.

However, our warrior was willing to go a lot further than any American athletics hero would go. Ludvigs made the ultimate sacrifice for a heterosexual man: he sacrificed his ass, literally.

After having tried out countless traditional remedies, and several less traditional ones, Per-Ove was finally presented with a bizarre suggestion. One of the doctors knew of a kind of healer who lived in the deep forests south of Oslo. He was quite an eccentric, but he also had a remarkably good track record. This was just before Christmas, and Per-Ove was sent over to him for a week's treatment. He brought no phone with him, and he was lodged in a basic camping cabin, literally in the middle of a Hansel and Gretel kind of forest. Every day, at set times, he went over to a main building some distance away from his cabin. This was where the miracle man lived. Every day that week, the treatment he underwent consisted solely of the following:

Per-Ove had to position his high and gangling body on all fours on a dinner table. Stark naked. For one hour he had an unknown, and probably raving mad, man's finger poking around inside his behind. I can only imagine what went through Ludvigs' head during those sessions. And to make it even worse, he was totally isolated from the rest of the world in between the sessions. I imagine hard, lonely nights in the small cabin. Nevertheless, he clenched his teeth and went on with it like a warrior. Needless to say, it didn't help his knees one bit, but I can guarantee you that no Norwegian football player has ever sacrificed himself for his club to the same degree. It is a rare thing to be emotionally touched by imagining a man being fingered in the ass by a lunatic from the deep forests. Very rare indeed.

The strange thing is that Martin Andresen – at one point Norway's most valuable player – used the same treatment throughout his entire career. He even had a finger man flown in to Bergen just before an important Brann match in their gold season 2007. I don't know much about whether he was injured or not. But it clearly did him no harm. Martin was the king of Brann Station.

Only days after Per-Ove had become official partner in my agency, I went for a trip to Oslo. I had a few meetings during the day, and Stig Torbjørnsen had invited me for dinner at night. Stig was a kind of agent slash adviser and broker for the big transfers into and out of Norway. Most of all he looked like a surfer. With his half-long looks-like-I-haven't-styled-it-styled hair and tanned skin, he could have jumped right out of his suit and into a pair of Billabong shorts and looked at home. He is quite a character, living in the snobbish west end of Oslo, with two things on his mind: football and racks. Not the Ikea kind, but the female kind. He loves racks. Like I do. So we had a lot to talk about that night.

I assumed early on, and know for sure today, that Stig Torbjørnsen is the number one person in Norway when it comes to spotting talent and quality. Some of his skills are probably inherited, some learned, but most of all it's due to his ability to watch two to four football matches every day, year-round; not just on TV, but preferably live. And in all corners of the world, often in Africa. He knew all there was to know about just about everything in the world of football, and I have often consulted him about players. A normal SMS correspondence between us could go like this:

– *Stig, do you know the young Moroccan who plays in French 2nd div? Dortmund had their eyes on him a few years back, and he played some good matches in the u-17 Africa Cup of Nations 5 years ago. Forgot his name. But is he premier league material?*

– *Knut, I watched him as recently as September this year. He is no good. BTW his name is Chivy, hehe. Cheers, The rack-meister.*

Stig is a damn likeable guy, and my respect for the Rosenborg management went up a notch when they did the smart move to hire him as talent scout. That turned out to be a wise decision. Now Stig had a smoking hot tip for me.

He told me about an Oslo boy he had followed since the player was a kid, who he was convinced that he was going to be brilliant. According to him, the only reason he hadn't had his breakthrough yet, was his lazy attitude. He didn't give a damn about anything and lacked focus and direction. Not grown up yet.

– But if he sorts himself out, he could become Norway's best player. And he is looking for an agent. I can fix it so you become his agent.

Here my lacking ability to judge talent kicked in. You see, as agent you are contacted daily by players, other agents or family members who want to introduce you to their player – usually "world class", of course. When you have to assess 500–1000 applications like that per year – and you do have to do that, because it is likely that five to ten of them have real qualities and potential – you need a trained eye.

I pulled the ace out of my sleeve – the legend and my childhood hero from Fyllingsdalen.

– *Wait a sec*, I told Stig, and called Per-Ove.

– *Hi Ludvigs. Stig Torbjørnsen recommends us to become agent for a player; I wondered if you knew him. His name is Mohammed Abdellaoue, or Moa, and he plays for Skeid. Any idea?*

– *Have seen him, not good enough*, Ludvigs replied.

I told Stig *"no, thank you"*.

Brilliant! I thought. Ludvigs is worth his weight in gold. Per-Ove and I, the perfect duo.

Two years later Moa was sold for 1.3 million euros to Hannover in the Bundesliga, with an agent fee of at least 130,000 euros.

After this first slip, Ludvigs arranged several of our largest and most profitable deals, including Anders Lindegaard to Aalesund and Nikola Djurdjic to Haugesund.

We travelled a lot, in Norway and the rest of Europe. It was a time of many experiences and lots of meetings with new people and players. And it was fun all the time, for behind his large snout and stern look, Ludvigs is a very funny guy, in fact a closet comedian. I remember particularly well a tour we had in the Balkans in car. We drove around for about a week in Serbia, Bosnia, Macedonia, Montenegro and Albania. The three last days of the trip Per-Ove decided he would only talk in rhyme, using a particular verse system. He even rhymed in English, both to the contacts we met and the people working at the hotels where we stayed.

We always booked moderately priced hotels, and always a double room. Per-Ove too has a sober-minded and sensible view on economics. I usually did the booking, and I often called him *Per-Ove Aru Kneehurt* when I booked. It never failed when the reception clerk hesitatingly said "*Welcome to our hotel, Mr. Aru Kneehurt*". It always got Ludvigs angry.

Cheap double rooms often means narrow double beds, and it took some time before it felt natural to lie spooning my old hero from Brann. However, it did feel very safe, that's for sure. The first night I was suddenly woken up by a sleep-headed Per-Ove pulling and tugging my pillow. After a short tug of war, which he won, I had no pillow under my head anymore. Instead, it was safely placed between Ludvigs' knees, who smacked his lips contently and slept on. That's how I discovered that most hotel rooms have an extra pillow in some closet or drawer.

It's the least I could do for my childhood hero with war-injured knees.

PER-OVE'S SECRET COMPANY

Since my beloved Brann started out in 1908, it's been as if some kind of curse followed them. The ancient Iranian religion of Zarathustraism believes in a demon and lord of destruction and chaos – Angra Mainyu – and I am starting to wonder if this demon is an always present and invisible member of the board at SK Brann. That demon had an important role in the game that ended with Per-Ove leaving Brann and joining as my co-partner.

It was in connection with Migen Memelli's mentioned transfer to Brann in early spring 2006 that Per-Ove and I started to get on well together. At that point, Per-Ove had been Director of Football in Brann since 2002 – the year he put his football boots of the shelf for good after 132 mandatory matches for Brann in a span of eight years. Obviously, the supporters felt sad about him finishing his career, but Per-Ove's knees hoisted the flag and rejoiced. The only job they had now, was to stabilize his bow-leggedness. The thing is that Per-Ove has an incredibly funny normal stance. He is high, rather slim, and has the kind of body that places any surplus fat exclusively in a capsule about the size of half a football in the middle of his belly. When he is standing up, although *up* may be to stretch it a bit, his pads are placed a small distance from each other, with his tootsies pointing diagonally to each side. His knees have a pronounced bend, not unlike the lot frequenting Plata by Oslo S – the city's main marketplace for highly unregulated substances. The gap between his legs form an egg-like shape from his flat feet to his nuts. His belly protrudes, with his back a bit crooked and his head slightly stooping. Often with both hands in his trouser pockets. But he doesn't just stand there. It's a constant swaying of knees, hips, back and neck. He is very much aware of it himself, but he can't do much about it except wishing that his entire football career never had taken place and made his body that rickety. Although nobody would really want that, not even the man himself. This may be a little harsh on Per-Ove, but it's far from the first time he's heard it from me. I have had a lot of fun pointing out his posture, and he always gets gloriously pissed off, with a little fox grin in the corner of his mouth.

His many years of experience and football knowledge, combined with his personal traits, were important factors in the unusual amounts of good player material that was brought to Brann during his years as Director of Football. Not only were the players good by themselves; more importantly, they were the right combination, both of player types and personalities. One factor is the combination of player skills on a team. Another, and in my opinion just as important, is the combination of personalities. Teams with too many similar personalities are rarely successful.

Any team should have a handful of anonymous hard workers; those who start each match, but are never mentioned in the papers the next day. They tend to run more than anyone else, are stable in their performance, and contribute to make their teammates good. Most of them are one hundred percent loyal to their employers and are always on time to trainings, well rested.

Then there is the warrior, generally centre back or midfield anchor. He often gets a yellow card, gets more and more beaten up as the match advances, and plays with cuts in his head and rackety knees.

And, of course, the star, who either shines with number ten on his back as a spectacular dribbler, or the striker who scores goal after goal. He always has either a headband that constantly gets his attention, or a fancy hairdo that needs straightening after each heading, and more often than not some tattoos that are highly visible – even on cold autumn matches. Where these players roll up their long sleeves, the warriors and anonymous hard workers often play with gloves and tights. The stars get all the attention, both from the media and the women.

In my opinion, the most important role of all is the clown. No team wins the league without a real clown in their squad. He is the one who takes unorthodox decisions on the field and do the funny things, with or without the ball. Just as much to entertain the crowd as from a tactical football point of view. Many players are too engaged in the work they do on the field to pay much attention to the tens of thousands watching them. In interviews after the match they don't know if they were nervous before a penalty, or how the atmosphere during the match were, because tunnel vision and job focus blurs everything else from the point when the referee blows the whistle. You can often hear players state that they cannot remember much of what happened outside the white rectangle. Surely it's a good thing that men who are paid hundreds of thousands a year to play 35 matches of 90 minutes each, have their full attention on their tasks. But if a team lacks a clown, it also lacks the communication between the players and the crowd. After all, the supporters are the ones paying their wages.

The clown is the one who pulls it all down to a homely level, and reminds the audience that they aren't machines out there on the field, but human beings. He shows both joy and sorrow, in sync with the crowd's state of mind. When a team lacks the clown, it is easy to see how starved the supporters are for attention from and engagement with the team. In those cases the audience monster can greedily accept even a hardly visible gesture from one of the players towards the crowd, and cheer wildly back in joy over having been seen and acknowledged. If you, in addition to the clown, season the squad with an appropriately crazy goalkeeper, the coach gets a perfectly balanced material to work with. A football myth is that number 1 and number 11 on a team are crazy. Number 1 is the goalkeeper and number 11 is traditionally the left forward in a 4-4-2 formation.

Both Charlie Miller and Erik Huseklepp fit into the category of clown, especially Miller. Raymond Kvisvik was a purebred clown. Mini Jacobsen, Steffen Iversen and Magne Hoseth are other examples. Players their home supporters love to acclaim, and the away supporters love to mock. Steffen Iversen, son of the old football celebrity Odd Iversen, had to get used to hearing the away supporters singing – *Son of a boozer, a-a-a, son of a boozer; son of a booooozer, a-a-a son of a boozer*, to the tune of *Guantanamera*.

Magne Hoseth, famous for his peculiar, and effeminate, running style, got – *For this is Hoseth running, and Hoseth runs like this. And this is Hoseth running, and Hoseth runs like this*, to the tune of a traditional

Nordic children's song that makes fun of an old aunt and how she moves her body when she walks. Iversen didn't take the mockery well, and it often made him angry and sad. Probably because they hit a sore spot. Steffen channelled his anger into his body's power reserves, and ended up being Norway's top scoring striker at the time. Magne Hoseth, on the other hand, received his song with humour, and ran towards the away supporters in an over-effeminate way with his arm swinging silly on one side, as if he were carrying a small handbag. Thus, he killed the song and made the away supporters burst in spontaneous laughter and applause over his lack of self-importance.

It's moments like this people talk about on their way home from a match. Interaction with the supporters – damn important!

Per-Ove excelled in thinking long term and big picture when he chose which players the Brann coach would have at his disposal. Here are a few of the best and most important signings Per-Ove did in his time as Director of Football:

In the category Money Machines I would like to mention Seyi Olofinjana, the man Per-Ove got Brann for free, where he played brilliantly. After only 34 matches, he was sold to Wolverhampton Wanderers in 2004 for almost 2.5 million euros. In the same category is Paul Scharner, a player Per-Ove had so much faith in that he paid 650,000 euros to get him from Red Bull Salzburg. 32 matches later, Scharner was sold on to Wigen Athletic for almost 4 million euros.

Of the type crowd favourites, Per-Ove signed among others Charlie Miller, the Scotsman who could create magic from nothing on the field. Always smiling and kind – never turned down a party. It wasn't a big secret that he often drank at least 12 shandies before he went to bed the night before a match.

Another player the crowd loved was Erik Huseklepp from Fyllingsdalen. Many of the city's propagators of The Law of Jante were sceptical to having a local player in Brann, but Per-Ove forced him through. Huseklepp played his first match against Fredrikstad in August 2005 and scored after 19 seconds, with his first kick on the ball. Talk about gagging the city troll! He was brought to Brann for small change, who later sold him to AS Bari in Italy for around 2 million euros.

Not to forget Raymond Kvisvik, the happy lad from Østfold who didn't exactly make you think of a professional football player when you saw him, with his flabby and plump body. However, he more than made up for it with his lovely dribbling and even lovelier clowning with the crowd.

Signing in Martin Andresen was another one of Per-Ove's great successes. Andresen was king from day one, and lifted Brann several notches. Outside the field, he is a calm, smiling guy. On the grass, he is crazy. Classic captain material. And he was extremely expensive. By far the stiffest-priced of Per-Ove's signings. Brann had to pay Stabæk 1.5 million euros. Moreover, Brann didn't get this money back when Martin snuck over to arch-competitor Vålerenga after his contract had ended. On the other hand, you cannot put a price tag on a league gold when Bergen hadn't seen the most precious metals since 1963.

Mons Ivar Mjelde took much of the glory for the gold in 2007, while the assistant coaches, and particularly Per-Ove Ludvigsen, were left behind in the shadows. Much of the player material Mons Ivar had at his disposal, was solely due to Per-Ove's work and skills. Without that the gold would never had happened.

Poor Roald Bruun-Hanssen who became Per-Ove's successor. Jumping after Wirkola – an idiom expressing the added difficulty of excelling at something when someone extremely good at it did it just before you – is a piece of cake compared to the job Roald had coming. And he got burned almost immediately. As agent in my firm, Per-Ove was asked to sell in the Swedish striker Joakim Sjöhage to Brann. Per-Ove watched the boy in a match, and concluded quickly that he wasn't close to being able to fight for a place on Brann's first-team squad. Being the shop man, I asked Per-Ove to sell him in anyway. Damn it, it was the job of Brann's athletics team to assess the player! I also reminded Per-Ove that he was on the other side of the table now, and had to turn around his way of thinking 180 degrees.

"No fucking way, Knut!", he replied fiercely. *"Dammit I am not promoting something I don't support myself, no matter what Brann thinks. This player is an embarrassment to introduce, and when Brann see the boy, they will quickly see it the way I do, that this is garbage, and I would have lost my credibility as agent for all foreseeable future. No, dammit! You and I, Knut, we are going to be one hundred percent different from all the other agents who come dragging in tons of players claiming they are all world class. I used to hate agents like that when I was Director of Football, and there is no way I am going to turn into one of them. You and I are going to be unanimous and agree*

one hundred percent every fucking time before we introduce a player to a club. We are ONLY going to promote quality. That is going to make the clubs' confidence in us grow over time, so that every time we call them to recommend a player, they will listen to us with both ears. See my point? That's how we are going to do it, end of discussion!'

I understood his point perfectly, but I had also brought Per-Ove into my firm, and I was paying him a higher salary than I had myself. Moreover, we had lots of travel expenses, office expenses and last, but not least, phone expenses. It was not unusual for us to get a monthly phone bill of 1500–2000 euros per head. Or rather, mine was always larger, often two–three times larger than Per-Ove's. He didn't like to talk on the phone, nor the selling or relation-building bit. The diplomacy and ass-kissing which is a necessary evil in this business. I excelled in that area. There were times when it got so bad that I had an ugly rash from my nickel allergy, on both cheeks, from a small metal button in the middle of the keypad on my phone. And I had to bring my charger with me everywhere.

So even if I agreed completely with Per-Ove in principle about our profile as an agent company, I had seen enough of mind-blowingly shocking signings of bullshit players in various clubs, with solid agent fees. After all, it was the athletics team in each club who had the damn responsibility for signing a player or not signing him. Nevertheless, I kept my mouth shut, and we gave up our exclusive right to represent Sjöhage. A few days later Brann signed the very same Joakim Sjöhage via another agent; they even paid well over 300,000 euros to his Swedish club Elfsborg. Per-Ove sighed deeply – resigned to the acquisition on behalf of Brann. I too sighed, but more on behalf of ourselves.

Sjöhage was an epic fail and a very embarrassing affair for Brann. He hardly played a match during an entire year, and Brann sent him back to Sweden with his tail between his legs, leaving a hole in Brann's bank account and a black stain on their athletics management.

Per-Ove officially resigned from Brann in November 2006. After a gradual transition, he was working full-time with me in January 2007. The backdrop for Per-Ove's resignation from Brann was a long-lasting and partly bitter conflict between Per-Ove and coach Mons Ivar Mjelde. And the fact that Per-Ove never confirmed this conflict in public, demonstrates what kind of man he is. In my opinion.

There was absolutely no communication, nada, zip, between any links in the athletics management chain. There is only one way to fix a situation like that when it has been going on for a long time: heads must roll. Besides, the conflict was becoming obvious to the rest of the club, and the bad energy was spreading through the corridors. The club was suffocating from within. This is my version of the story, and other parties will have their own, different versions. Espen Steffensen said it well: if you were to ask twelve people who worked in Brann at the time, you would get twelve different stories about what happened in 2006.

However, Brann's talent developer, Kjetil Knutsen, and their analysis manager, Robert Hauge, were both loyal Per-Ove supporters. Together we started an investment company that we hoped would give us all a good yield on our investments, among other things in real estate in the Balkans. But regardless of how promising the projects might have seemed, they would not give us food on the table in the near future. We all needed a job to provide for our families, so we decided on the following:

Per-Ove and I would manage the agent company, in which my dad too had a share. This was a pure agent enterprise that would provide our monthly pay. Everything we gained or lost in this company was shared between Per-Ove and me, plus a little to my dad.

In addition, we founded a company that was solely an investment company, with six co-owners: Per-Ove, dad, Kjetil, Robert, my brother and I. All had equal shares and each invested the same amount, 12,500 euros, which gave a total capital of 75,000 euros. We reckoned that would cover the company's expenses for one to two years. That is the time we gave ourselves to make something happen. Per-Ove and I would do the main share of the work in the investment company, but we could ask the others for assistance if necessary.

Per-Ove had made his decision; he was all-in. Kjetil and Robert had much greater doubts about whether we would make any money in this company, and whether they would be able find some sensible work while *waiting* to get rich. First milestone was to hire Kjetil in to the company full-time as soon as some cash started to materialise.

Kjetil, Robert and Per-Ove decided after some time that they should go one for all, all for one. The three musketeers. Per-Ove was the first one who, to the city's great surprise, announced that he withdrew from his positions in Brann with immediate effect. Everyone wondered why. Instead of bitching about unfair treatment and conflict with Mjelde in the media, he turned the other cheek and claimed he withdrew because of the bad results that autumn; that it was his duty to leave the helm to someone else. The media didn't quite buy it; this was too uncommon in Norwegian football – the opposite of the normal, which would be to cling on to your position to the bitter end. However, no matter how much they interrogated him, he stuck with his story.

Then it was Kjetil's and Robert's turn. Together they agreed on when they should deliver their resignation to Brann, and hopefully get a severance package that could keep them afloat until they found another job.

A week later, a newspaper in Bergen had the following headline:

Per-Ove's secret company

The newspaper had discovered that the six of us had started a company together. In other words, they had stumbled upon the investment company, not the agent company. They took it for granted that the company was about selling players, and Brann's manager was challenged to answer how they felt about two of their employees being co-partners in a company that promoted players. He told them, correctly enough, and according to the unambiguous FIFA regulations on this subject, that the two activities weren't compatible. Assuming this was correct, the two had either to leave Brann or withdraw completely from the company. My father assured the newspaper that this company in no way were to be involved in promoting or selling players. After an e-mail and following phone call with both Brann's manager and the newspaper, the case was declared null and void. Nothing censurable.

The strange thing is that both Ole Gunnar Solskjær and Eirik Bakke had significant owner interests in the agent company of Prins Charming Himself, the self-declared Norwegian Agent King, player agent Jim Solbakken. That ownership arrangement didn't just violate the FIFA regulations grossly; it's probably a violation of Norwegian corruption laws as well. It's definitely serious, in any case. Moreover, when it was discovered by accident, nobody pointed as much as a finger at either Jimmyboy, The Baby-faced Assassin or No Way Bakke. They should have been suspended all three of them, and Solbakken should have been heavily fined and deprived of his agent license. However, these lads are still running their business as if nothing happened. While Solskjær was coach for Molde, Jim Solbakken was agent for nine of the players in the club, plus he was agent for Solskjær! That in itself is reason enough to lose your license, according to the rules, but nothing happens. British newspapers reacted strongly when it turned out that Solskjær in the weeks after he became coach for Cardiff, fetched one player after another. The reason they reacted was that all the players had the same agent as Solskjær himself: Jimmyboy. All right, perhaps I'm a little envious of their success and the money they make. But what a filthy bunch!

NOTHING GLAMOROUS

One of the first things we had to do as an agency was to find an office. We didn't need anything fancy, because we rarely ever had any visiting customers or clients – we visited them. So it suited us perfectly when some acquaintances fixed us up with a room on the ground floor of an old city block. There were four rooms there with a common entrance, and our neighbours were a janitor, a vacuum cleaner salesman and an accountant. The four of us also had access to a really grim loo in the basement, which was never cleaned and lacked necessities like paper and soap. Us being men, that's how it was and that's how it stayed. Our office was two times four metres, and the desks another buddy had given us, fit perfectly next to each other to make one long desk where we both could sit. To keep our work a bit organized, we tried to turn up no later than nine each morning.

After a month or two, we had many balls in the air and enough to do. For an agent there are normally ten cases in play that you almost land, before you actually land one. Since you don't know which the successful one is, you have to keep the pressure up on all of them. You learn as you go, of course, and after a while, you get better at prioritizing based on probabilities. In the beginning, we could not be picky in any way; the competition in this business is extremely fierce. We each bought a second-hand laptop online. To sum it up, you could say that being a football agent isn't always that damn glamorous; it's hard work like everything else, and you have to penny- pinch to make it work. Per-Ove was the wiser of us when it came to spending money. He always stopped and asked if it was really necessary to buy this or that. A normal day at the office could consist of me making lots of calls to clubs and agents, while Per-Ove handled the incoming mail – mainly resumes from players. Many agents had streaming services they gave us login credentials to, where we could access archives and fetch football matches where the players presented to us, had been playing. Watching matches occupied a large part of Per-Ove's day. After each match he noted his assessment of the player with regards to various criteria, and summed it up by categorizing the player in one of three categories: *Tippeligaen* – the Norwegian equivalent of Premier League; *Adeccoligaen* – the Norwegian 1st Division (now rebranded as *OBOS-ligaen)*; or *Not good enough*. Then I introduced the player to a club, where most of them asked at a fairly early stage whether I had seen him playing. It gave the extra authority that mattered to be able to say that Per-Ove had watched him in two matches, and then relate the player's strong and weak points. It worked very well.

That was another rule we had – always to be up-front about the player's weak points, as well as his strong ones. Most of our competitors presented an idealized version of their candidates: good at everything on the field, fantastic personality. Even if everybody knows that there is no such thing as a flawless player, at least not on premier league level. So, when we presented a forward, we would for instance tell them about strong aspects like extreme speed and strength behind the defenders, in addition to being able to shoot well with both legs. Weaknesses could be that he played lousy as first defender and was a bit unfit, and that he could be a troublemaker outside the field. When you play your cards up-front like this, the club has a much better chance of making a correct judgement of a player's strong sides versus his weak ones. It was a completely new thing for agents to do this, and we got very positive feedback to our honesty. We did lose a few sales because of it, but we still felt it was the right way to go about things.

With our different personality traits and skills, we complemented each other well, and we were both very happy with how the work was divvyed up. However, gradually it became obvious that both of us lacked one property that is crucial no matter what business you're in: structure. Per-Ove and I are both completely devoid of it. No trace whatsoever. We made all-out efforts from time to time, and promised ourselves we would shape up – but it didn't last for more than a few minutes. As our index file grew and we had more and more balls in the air at the same time, this became a serious problem for us. We managed our time poorly, spent energy on nonsense, and lost several sales, simply because we weren't organized enough. I fantasized about hiring an economics student in a half-time position – someone who were starving to get to work and had all the right skills and traits. We talked a bit about it, and I thought it would pay off quickly. But I also had a great deal of respect for my former football hero, and he usually got the last word. We didn't have the economy to hire anyone else.

In addition to all the mails we received all the time from agents and players from around the world, we regularly got applications from football-loving fellow citizens. These were simply people who would like to get into the business, and wondered if we needed an assistant. In several cases, these were obviously qualified people with a wide experience, but we didn't have the budget for it, so they mostly got polite rejections and wishes of good luck. On one occasion, we were very close to getting Vålerenga coach Petter Myhre on our team. The plan was that he should handle everything in the eastern parts of the country. We nearly closed the deal, but in the last second TV2 stepped in and snatched him from under our noses.

Then one day an application dumped into our mailbox that stood out from the crowd. It was a young fellow from Tromsø, with the name of Roald Øien.

What he wrote resonated with us, especially the part about his abilities to work in a structured manner. We talked on the phone, and he made a sufficiently solid impression for us to buy him a ticket to Bergen. He had a different personality than Per-Ove and me. Moreover, he was really adept at coding, programming and anything that had to do with computers. At least compared to us, who were both in the Bronze Age when it came to computing. We told him, truthfully, that we really liked him, but that we didn't have a penny to spare at the moment. That wasn't a problem for Roald; money was far from the top of his list. He genuinely wanted to make something happen, something new and big. He was like manna from heaven for us, and after a short time, we had completely new office routines with good flow and a good overview. Roald designed systems and prepared things in a better way for the accountant so they would spend less time, and less of our money. Besides, he wasn't afraid of making calls to clubs, agents or players. Not at all. I don't know how many hours of brilliant work this man did for us without compensation, but I am guessing close to a thousand.

The fact that Roald came in gave us the opportunity to spend more time in the field while he was managing the office. So we travelled a lot, mainly in Europe. We built networks and established contacts. Once a year we did a tour in the southern part of Norway to visit the football clubs there. Great experience! We started from Bergen down the west coast to Haugesund, Stavanger, Kristiansand, Skien, and then crisscrossing eastern Norway. The coach of Moss Fotballklubb at that time, Geir Bakke, ended up inviting us home for dinner. That's the stuff long-lasting contacts are made of.

When our office building was sold, we moved into a 100 square meters (1100 square feet) flat downtown. I got it cheap from a buddy who had been granted a trial permission to move back in with his wife, after they separated a year earlier. He wanted to hang on to the flat as an escape hatch, in case it didn't work out, and it suited us all perfectly. This was a palace compared to our first office, and we had a great time there – until a player we had sold in to Bergen needed a place to stay for himself and his pregnant wife. He didn't have any money and was desperate. We gave them the flat, and that was it.

Per-Ove had recently built himself a new house, so our new office became the basement apartment there. Short commute for Ludvigsen. And that was a good thing, because our company was growing now, and we had increasingly more to do. We were where we were supposed to be. And the only way was up, right?

THE BEST AGENT IN THE WORLD

Migen Memelli had played one year for Brann. Unfortunately, he hadn't become the success we all had hoped. And that really sucked, because both the supporters and coach Mons Ivar loved him. It was love at first kick of the ball. I still remember his first appearance in April 2007, when he took an almost packed Brann Stadion by storm.

A few minutes before the match ended, at 1–1 against Lillestrøm, he was substituted into the match. To me in the crowd it was a big moment when I, for the first time, could contribute to my own team, Brann, as an agent – when Migen pulled on the red Brann suit with the number 25 on his back.

He exploded out onto the field as if he was Usain Bolt starting his hundred-meter race. Brann played 4-4-2, and now it was Migen's turn to find his place in the formation. He was designated to be one of the two-man forward team, with Bengt Sæternes as his partner.

However, Migen wasn't quite able to feel at home. He did run up in the space where he was supposed to go, but when he didn't get the ball at once, he started waving his arms madly and yelling like a pee-wee player on a sandlot. He was over-excited and continued to run back and forth to make himself playable. It looked pretty weird, and the crowd cheered and applauded his eagerness. After having played two–three minutes and covered around half a mile of sprinting, Migen was visibly frustrated by not having had the ball at his feet even once. You could practically see him thinking that this wasn't worth the trouble. He left his space and started a mad sprint diagonally backwards on the field. The ball was in play down by Brann's corner flag, where Lillestrøm's wing were challenging Brann's back.

The Lillestrøm wing had his gaze at the back and at the goal, and was totally unprepared for that the opponent's newly acquired Albanian forward might come dashing in from the opposite corner flag on the other side of the field – literally the longest possible distance between two points on a football field. Migen came like a raging bull with hatred in his eyes, and all the cells in his body had only one single thing on the agenda: we are getting that bloody ball! The back player wasn't aware of Migen until the distance between them had become around ten meters, and it was as if his entire Lillestrøm body instinctively knew that there was only one sensible thing to do now – get out of the way. So he did. Migen captured the ball promptly, turned around, and drove the ball up the other way like a locomotive.

The home crowd had already noticed the incident when Migen started his run, and they cheered as if he had scored when he snatched the ball. Now they cheered him onwards on the field. He passed two men and crossed the halfway line. Two other Lillestrøm players were heading towards him at full speed and with an obvious plan. Migen looked up, realized that it would be hard to dodge them, looked at the goal, forty meters, then at the ball. Bang! The horse kicked the ball so hard that if it had been filmed in super slow motion by the people at the Discovery Channel, you would probably have seen the ball becoming soft and wrap around Migen's boot like a sausage, before catching momentum and taking off towards the goal. Although *towards the goal* is somewhat misleading, because the ball landed way up in the crowd, behind the skilled LSK goalkeeper Heinz Müller. Nevertheless, the crowd rose and applauded. THIS was a real warrior. Now Migen was like a man completely out of role, space and control. He ran at maximum speed the whole time, always after the ball. He fought like a gladiator in his own defence zone, ran long runs along the side like a wing, fought in the air like a midfield anchor, and shot at the goal from all angles. He covered nearly all roles on the field; the only one he didn't do was goalie. Mons Ivar yelled from the sideline, and gesticulated feverishly to Migen to get him back where he belonged. But Migen didn't listen, and Mjelde gave up after a while, threw his arms expressively forward, shook his head, made a U-turn and went back to his coach seat: this was just going to have to play out.

And the crowd singing, at the tune of *You are my sunshine*, over and over, to the lunatic on the grass field:

We have Memelli, Migen Memelli
He dribbles any and everyone
We always win when Memelli puts it
So come and sing for Migen again
Shalalalala Oh
Shalalalala Oh

Migen's incredible enthusiasm was contagious, not only to the crowd but to his team as well. The entire Brann squad raised the frequency a notch, and Lillestrøm was under a great deal of pressure. Then the moment came.

A moment like this one is a culmination of events leading up to it; it's a moment you dream of, and that creates stories starting with *Do you remember that match?* The stadium clock had passed 90 minutes, and the match was well into the added time with only seconds left to play. Migen happened to be more or less where he was supposed to be – close to the opponent's goal. Bengt Sæternes managed to turn the right way and lifted the ball into Lillestrøm's penalty field. Frode Kippe, normally solid as a rock, miscalculated completely and the ball went in an arc over him. Right at Migen, who received it with his chest and positioned it perfectly at his own right foot, all alone against Heinz Müller. It was virtually a ready-scored goal, and the crowd cheered in anticipation of the sound of the ball hitting the net the next second. Mjelde was already down in knee stance, ready to take his customary celebration jump when Brann scored, with a fist stretched against the sky. All Migen needed to do was to roll the ball calmly passed Müller's wide-open left side. But Migen's legs weren't calibrated for accurate placing of the ball or light inside touching this evening; in his head everything was on fire. He fired off the ball with full power. The ball went like a cannonball straight towards the net, but directed at exactly the zone where it couldn't pass. Goalkeeper Müller was hit so hard and unexpectedly that you could hardly call it a save. But he had to position his 193 centimetre high body somewhere – a body with several years' experience from the German Bundesliga. The bullet ricocheted from Müller and out.

– NOOOOOOOOOOOO!!!!!

The wailing scream of deep, shocking disappointment that resounded from Brann Stadion when Migen missed, was so loud my mom could probably hear it on the balcony of her house, regardless of the wind direction.

The headline in the newspaper Bergensavisen the next day was *Migen should have scored. He didn't need to shoot in 150 there!* quoted from Mons Ivar Mjelde. The understatement of the day. According to Lillestrøm's coach, Uwe Rösler, there was one particular reason why Migen didn't score. You would probably expect him to continue by saying that that one reason was their goalkeeper , Heinz Müller. But no – Rösler was convinced that Lillestrøm had *help from God.*

Later that night I met Migen home at his flat. I'd managed to lodge him in a three bedroom flat with panoramic view over downtown. It was situated in the best part of Bergen's version of Beverly Hills – Fjellsiden. The owner of the flat was a devoted Brann supporter, and Migen paid little more than pocket lint in rent. The owner gave up at least 1200 euros a month to accommodate a Brann player. He hadn't gotten value for his money that night, and Migen himself looked like he had been cheated on, sitting submerged on a tatty, worn-out sofa I had helped him buy from a Salvation Army charity. Albanians don't spend money on unnecessary things; everything except a minimum for life support, is sent straight home to mom and dad. A nice counterweight to many high-flying new-rich football stars.

The small margin Migen so desperately needed on his side on overtime against Lillestrøm, kept eluding him through all his Tippeliga matches in 2006. His efforts were irreproachable, but the last millimetre was lacking. And with fierce competition over the forward positions that year, he usually started out on the bench. Only one match did he play from the start.

He got playing time in eighteen matches, and scored one lousy goal. Luckily, he had a great autumn both in the UEFA Cup and in the Royal League, where he will always be remembered in Brann.

When the season was over, and Brann were taking stock with us, we agreed that it was best for both parties if Migen got more playing time. Mons Ivar couldn't guarantee that, and Migen was put on the so-called transfer list. This is a summary of the players a club would consider letting go to another club, if the time, and money, were right. It wasn't that Migen had been a flop in Brann – far from it. There were a lot of interest from other, competing Tippeliga clubs, and we had talks with several of them. But Brann weren't that keen on letting him go to a competitor; after all nothing is worse than letting a player go and then watch him suddenly crack the code and start scoring like crazy, maybe even against Brann themselves. Mjelde had sufficient doubts about Migen that he would have preferred us to find a club outside of Norway. However, selling Migen out of Norway was easier said than done. On the paper, he was a benchwarmer who didn't score, and that's a crappy resume when you are selling a forward. Migen himself was frustrated and angry with Brann for depriving him of many good opportunities in Norway. I stuck to the rules of the game, but in reality I was every bit as frustrated as he was.

I sent out feelers through my network in east and west. Only silence in reply, until, out of the blue, a tiny door opened to a Swedish club. Albanian players had been very successful in Sweden for several years, so Memelli's name already had a good ring to it in Swedish ears. The Gothenburg club GAIS were on the lookout for a new centre forward – an exceptionally strong striker alone on top in a 4-5-1 formation. With his extreme physique, a crucial prerequisite for this forward role, their coach, Roland Nilsson, could tick off all the boxes on his form for Migen.

Migen was formally invited to Gothenburg for try-out in the end of March 2007. I had a meeting with Brann before the departure, and they told me that if GAIS like what they see, and make an offer, we would of course like to get back what we paid for Migen, that is 80,000 euros. If they are difficult, we will let him go for free, but don't play the first card.

To an agent this is a really nice message to bring in your luggage. They accept a price tag of zero, and anything above zero is pure bonus and a star in my agent resume. There was also a third party who had a share in any resale of Migen, but they had no right to influence Brann's negotiations. The third party was entitled to thirty percent of the transfer sum, after Brann's original costs were covered. In other words, 30% of anything over 80,000 euros.

In the world of football, it's a matter of course that in the situation Migen and Brann were in at that point, no club in the world would pay MORE than what Brann had paid originally. After all, Brann had assessed Migen beforehand and paid 80,000 expecting him to score goals. When it turned out that he didn't score as anticipated, played little throughout the year, and Brann came to the conclusion that he needed to find another club, it goes without saying that Brann couldn't demand double what they had paid themselves. It wouldn't make any sense, and the discussion in a setting like that will always be how much less than the original price the buying club is willing to offer. So I wasn't concerned about the negotiations between the clubs, but the salary negotiations might become challenging. The salaries were substantially lower in Sweden than in Norway, and even if Migen only made an average 100,000 euros gross a year, I saw a potential Gordian knot there, but only a small one.

It is not unusual with mid-season transfers to have a gentlemen's agreement between the clubs that the player in question shouldn't be part of the squad in the next match between the two teams. The rest of the Brann team were in Stavanger to play against Viking, while we flew to Gothenburg via Copenhagen, and were well received when we landed at Landvetter Airport Sunday night. We were lodged downtown. The next morning we were taken to the training field, idyllically situated with forest on all sides. Migen did a couple of training sessions, and made a fair impression. However, it was far from enough to form a basis for a buy or no-buy decision by Coach Roland Nilsson. He was fairly young at the time, with longish, blond hair. Nilsson had his breakthrough as coach for GAIS, and moved on from there to Malmö FF with great success, and on again to F.C. Copenhagen, where he ended up being pushed out by Ståle Solbakken.

Memelli's golden opportunity to convince the demanding Swedes came the next day, when GAIS were playing an away match against Elfsborg, on their brand new and very impressive stadium. It was of course a training match; otherwise, Migen couldn't have played, given that his player's license was still on the desk of the Director of Football on Brann Stadion.

I was directed to a seat and introduced to the guy sitting next to me. He turned out to be the main investor in GAIS and owner of the Swedish branch of INTERSPORT. In other words, the guy with the moneybag, and his opinions about Memelli's skills would weigh just as much as Roland Nilsson's, if not more. He was a sturdy man, dressed as if on his way to a British foxhunt. Very likeable, and we chatted unrestrainedly during the warmup.

I talked a lot with Migen before the match, and emphasized the importance of making himself noticed quickly. I wanted him to find back to the feeling he had as the bull in the stall in the 78th minute on Brann Stadion the year before. Migen wasn't hard to ask.

He ruled on the field in front of more or less two thousand spectators who had come to see the match, or probably just as much to see the new Borås Arena. He kept winning duels and managed to create many chances. However, the curse seemed to have sneaked into his luggage over to Sweden; the ball kept eluding the goal. Still, the foxhunter was visibly impressed, and talked warmly about him at my side. I hoped the coach down at the bench had similar thoughts. Then, in the sixtieth minute, it finally happened. Migen slammed the ball in the net ceiling with a volley, and in the same moment I could see by the body posture of my neighbour that the decision had been made, and he was already preparing for the next phase; the negotiations. Now we both needed to change hats immediately to avoid being caught off-guard. Game on.

Shortly thereafter Migen got his second yellow card for the day, and walked off the field with the referee's red card high in the air behind his disappointed back. But he had no reason to be disappointed; the Intersport owner had just skipped the entire hat changing game. He put all his cards on the table and said, *I want him for GAIS*. He wondered where we lived, and told me a car would pick us up at the hotel the next day, so we could discuss the economy comfortably over a lunch. Perfect, I thought, apparently Mr. Nilsson's opinion didn't weight heavily here. The man with the foxy clothes calls the shots.

At the hotel that night I had to follow standard procedure in situations like this one; I had to talk down Migen's expectations, and make sure he went to bed hoping that I would be able to negotiate a deal the next day, and that if the offer was 70,000 euros, that would be great. It was a bit less than he had, but on the other hand, the taxes were lower here, not to mention the prices of food, lodging, and etcetera. In summary, he got my message and understood my calculations – that even with a somewhat lower wage in Sweden he would end up better off.

The car came to pick us up as agreed – a black Mercedes Benz with a suited driver behind the wheel. He uttered a few pleasantries, but other than that, didn't say a word the half hour it took to reach our destination. A huge wrought-iron gate blocked the entry to a tree-lined road that wound beautifully through a park. I caught a glimpse of a lake and parts of a building a few hundred meters inside the park. After a few seconds, the gate split in half, and we entered. Wow! What a place! It turned out to be the house of the sporting goods retailer. A house that was on the verge of being a small castle, beautifully situated by the idyllic lake. The owner met us on the driveway, dressed in shorts and Hawaii shirt, barefoot. I felt seriously overdressed in my tailor-made Ermenegildo Zegna suit, that I loved so much. Better over than under, I thought, and didn't spend more energy on that.

He had sent his missus and kids away for the occasion, so we had the house to ourselves. The slightly stiff posture the sheer pomposity of the place had given me, vanished like a fart in the wind when he showed me into the kitchen. It was large and lived-in, with a solid dinner table that looked like it was made of driftwood or something similar. Two large brass bowls were on the table. One was filled to the brim with newly cooked claws of king crab. The other was packed with various glass bottles of beer. He offered me a chair and handed me a table napkin.

– *Have you tried king crab with butter sauce? No? It's my favourite.*

He demonstrated the best way to eat them: take one claw in your own claw – they were already split along the middle – pour over butter sauce, and enjoy! With the rustic table as plate. The atmosphere was set. Lovely!

We talked about everything but football, and laughed a lot. After about an hour, he slammed his bear paws in the table, and said:

– *There. Now you have to tell me, how much is this going to cost?*

Straight to the point, just how I like it. Twice we threw the ball back and forth, about who should name an amount first. I knew Brann would applaud if I managed to get 80,000, but I had a gut feel, and definitely wanted him to shoot first.

– *Okay, Knut, 200,000. Straight cash. No complicated clauses or any other crap. Two hundred thousand, pure and simple.*

Luckily, I had finished eating; otherwise, I would probably have choked on the crab. I tried to keep up my poker face. Inside I was dancing of shock and joy. Think fast, Knut. When he opens with that amount, he obviously has more to offer. You never start with your maximum, right? I went all out, and said that's probably a bit lower than what Brann had in mind; that they wanted 350,000 euros. He didn't seem offended – more like thoughtful. Maybe I had overdone it.

My phone rang. It was an Oslo-based agent. He sounded stressed and asked if we had started the negotiations about Migen. I asked him how he was involved in that, and he told me he was to negotiate the transfer sum on behalf of Brann. He had read about the try-out online, and offered to help Brann. According to the rules, this was fair enough in a sense; as agent, I am not allowed to negotiate both the transfer sum and the player's personal contract. However, this was a deeply dormant rule, and it hadn't been a subject when I left Bergen.

The agent was already in the car on his way to Gothenburg, only a half hour's drive away. I went into another room to talk more privately, and to hear which amounts he and Brann had been talking about. Stupid as I am, I told him about the bid that was already on the table. He became frantic:

– *Take it, take it!! Don't fool around negotiating, just take it!!*

– *But, I definitely think…,* I tried.

– *You accept!* he interrupted me. *And … don't do anything else until I get there.*

I was a little confused and definitely jerked out of the good flow. I told the Swede that a representative from Brann was on his way. He shrugged and expressed that it wasn't any problem, but he couldn't quite see the point. To him that only meant higher costs.

The minutes passed, and we were both twinning our thumbs waiting for the agent to arrive. The Swede asked me, after having stared emptily out in the air for a few minutes, if I had good connections in Brann. I confirmed that I had.

– *What if we say 300,000. Still no clauses. What do you think of that?*

I knew very well what Brann would say to that. Not only would they sign the contract on its way out from the printer – they would also hoist a flag and hail me for outstanding work. But I didn't tell that to the Swede.

I defied the Oslo agent and called Brann directly. Sure, they knew that he was on his way, but were, like myself, puzzled and surprised about his intervention. I told them quickly that I had this under control, and that I might get the amount up to around 120,000. Brann thought I was joking, and rejoiced when they understood that I was being serious. No, they definitely didn't need any extra agent here; this was better than anyone had dreamt of. I smiled thinking about their reaction when they learned the real amount I had managed to get. In the same moment, the other agent arrived.

His name is Lars Petter Fosdahl, and we had already met on several occasions. I disliked him intensely. He reminds me a lot of the Harry Potter character Bartemius Crouch Jr, constantly licking his mouth with a serpent-like tongue. I shuddered, and the Swede didn't seem very happy either.

A sense of urgency arose when the serpent escorted us back and forth between the kitchen and the living room, one after the other, so he could talk to each of us one-to-one. A divide-and-conquer sort of thing. This can't possibly be in Brann's best interest, I thought, and pondered upon how to get out of this mess. The next time I was up for an audience with Bartemius, it was obvious that his reptile brain had cooked up some cunning scheme. It was crucial that Brann didn't know how much the Swede was willing to pay for Migen. I hadn't talked to Brann about that, right? I told him I had, and he sighed so stagy that the Swede grinned all the way over on the other side of the room, despite that he couldn't hear what we said. But when I told him I had said to them that the bid was at 120,000, his eyes glowed yellow again.

– *Ok, Knut. I'll handle the communication between the Swede and Brann from here. And you won't regret this – I promise you that. There is enough for everybody.*

There was no doubt what his plans were: one of the oldest tricks in the agent book – a trick Rune Hauge made his own in the nineties. Hauge was a master in sitting on both sides of the table in a negotiation, and it often ended with Hauge himself getting a large slice of the cake. Hauge probably did this many times, although only two of them are publicly known. When he sold Pål Lydersen from Start to Arsenal, one amount was stated to Start and another one to Arsenal. Both Hauge and Graham helped themselves to the unknown difference. Hauge was sentenced in this case to lose his license for all future, but the sentence was later moderated to only two years. Therefore, he could continue his role-play with a good margin when Eirik Bakke in 1999 went from Sogndal to Leeds for

5.5 million euros – at that time the second largest sum paid for a transfer from Norway. However, all this was some years back now, and it wasn't that easy to fool a club in 2006.

A smooth tongue would be needed to get the Swede on his side to get his money. I was brusquely shut out from the negotiation room, and after a short while, I heard the Swede raising his voice markedly in the neighbour room. I interpreted what was happening as an obvious fraud against Brann, but also against the third party who was entitled to thirty percent of everything above 80,000. If the transfer ended up at 300,000, thirty percent would be a rather large sum. I was less concerned about what the police would think of this than what the third party investor would do if the word got out that I was involved in trickery. From day one as agent, I had a clear goal of being honest and clean. *No way*, I thought. *No fucking way!*

While the arguing was at its worst in the next room, I called Brann. I told them the Swede had agreed to 300,000, and that was definitely his maximum. They were speechless, and it took a little while before they were able to say anything sensible in reply. They hadn't heard anything from Crouch Jr – hadn't he arrived yet? He had indeed, I told them, and he had made a bloody mess in the room just next to me. So be my guest if you want to deal with him, but I promise you that it will all go to hell then. I didn't go into more detail, and we hung up. A moment later, I heard a phone ring and the serpent answered. The door opened and the Swede came barging into the kitchen where I was. Angry as a bear. He didn't even look at me. In the middle of the living room I could see my colleague standing with the phone at his ear, listening and at the same time licking his mouth frantically. He turned around his own axis until he faced me, and set his gaze fiercely at me. If we had been in the world of Harry Potter, it would no doubt have killed me right there and then.

His conversation with Brann was over, and he joined us in the kitchen. His body passed me, with his head and gaze locked at me, and his neck turned almost 180 degrees before his tendons and muscles reached their physical limit. He whispered something to the Swede, who immediately transformed his posture and looked at me. But his gaze was warm and grateful. He understood, and winked at me. I knew I had made the right decision. The transfer amount landed on 300,000 – a bit less than my highest bid – and

Brann were ecstatic. The serpent that had entered the equation, remained Brann's problem; they were the ones who had hired him. Any share of the transfer sum was out of the question – that much was clear to them as well. Some experiences cost money, and Brann had that.

With the serpent out of the house, the bond between the Swede and me became if possible even better. With my actions, I had won the respect of the experienced businessman with his heart in GAIS. Now it was time to negotiate Migen's wages.

I was on cloud nine when I knocked on the door to Migen's hotel room a few hours later. Not only could I confirm that the clubs had agreed: on top of that, Migen would double his basic wage. PLUS various bonuses, that in effect could almost triple it. We danced in each other's arms, and Migen jumped in the bed of pure joy.

Then we packed and went to the clubhouse, where the contract, formulated as agreed, was waiting for us to sign it. No media, since the transfer at this point was a secret. All the secrecy that surrounds transfers is a strange thing that rarely is based on any logic. Only in cases where someone is afraid someone else can get their hands on a player, does it make any sense. Why make such a fuss about keeping quiet about something that is already signed and irreversible, regardless of how many know about it? This has always been an enigma to me, but since this kind of intel obviously means a lot to most football clubs, I had a hard rule about never talking to the press about anything. Ever! Nevertheless, I broke my own rule on our way to Gothenburg, when the fun, but cunning fox of a sports journalist Davy Wathne, fooled me during a stopover. He saw Migen and knew that he was supposed to be on the other side of the country – in Stavanger. So he wondered what was up. I gave him my usual *no comment*, and he told me to *relax* and *calm down*:

– *You can talk to me off the record, you know*, he continued.

– *And Knut, I am an old student friend of your father's. You can trust me.*

With his last argument, that a story about Migen being on his way to GAIS would have zero value, I lifted the veil a little. He said *Good luck, Migen*, and we boarded. Before we landed, it was already a story on TV. I don't blame him – I am the one who opened my mouth. He just did his job. Moreover, to the coming generation Davy Wathne is what Arne Scheie was to us. Every era needs one of those, who for better or for worse keep the enthusiasm for football alive in their country.

The cat was already out of the bag, so when Anders Pamer called from the newspaper Bergensavisen, it would just have been childish to deny everything. He got his interview, and in the story that went to print the next day, the following quote was included from a happily shouting Migen Memelli:

– *I have the best agent in the world!*

GAIS behaved decently, and Brann's money arrived according to the contract. It was my job to forward the share to the third party investor, who was abroad. The money would be in my possession for a short while, before the rightful owner received them as we had agreed.

The money had just arrived in Albania via telegraph, when a desperate Migen called me and told me his father was critically ill. He could only get the right treatment in Italy, and it was very expensive. Migen had sent all he had, but it wasn't enough. Without treatment, his father would die, and Migen knew that the money had a stopover with me before reaching the rightful owner.

– *Knut, please. He will die. I will pay it all back in a month or two.*

What could I say? Of course, Migen got all the money at once. I didn't see neither the money nor Migen until several years later, and then only Migen. We met for breakfast in a French café in Tirana. They have a marvellously good baker there, who makes wonderful cakes. What we talked about, is between us, but we said goodbye with a hug after an hour.

NETWORK

To be a successful football agent, you need several qualities. You must like talking to people, you must get used to getting doors slammed in your face (often), you must be prepared to test your own moral limits, and you must be ready to stand in the critical limelight of the media (often). Having knowledge about football, or even liking football, makes little difference, except that it makes the job more fun. A football agent's inventory and capital – what separates back alley cats from agents like Paul Stretford – is your network.

The network is the foundation of any agent enterprise. A dentist, doctor, hairdresser or catering company can build a large portfolio of customers and contacts. This portfolio has a real and saleable value.

Still, a brand new agency can't simply buy another agent's network. That would be like a person with no friends paying someone to take over some of his or her friends. Doesn't work.

No matter if you are rich and famous or a Joe Average – everyone has to start from scratch. So one of the most important tasks I did in my first years as an agent, was to travel and meet people. I established many contacts via phone and e-mail as well, but the people I met face to face, shook hands with, got drunk with – those connections were much stronger. I already had a vast network on the Balkans. I had entrance to all the clubs in Serbia, Croatia, Macedonia, Montenegro, Bosnia and Albania. In all these countries, except for Croatia, I also had good connections in the national football associations. Having an entrance to the association is worth its weight in gold when you want to move a player out of the country. I could have paper work that could normally take weeks to finish, completed in a day. Therefore, to distinguish myself from the other agents in Scandinavia, I tried to get the reputation of being the agent that *owned* the Balkans.

In 2006, Europe had started to notice players from the Balkans, when one after another from Croatia, Bosnia and Serbia was signed in large clubs like Manchester United, Chelsea, FC Porto, Inter Milan, Juventus and others. Everybody knows that these clubs know what they are doing, and that they don't burn millions without being close to hundred percent certain that the player is good enough. That is why the doubts, which had been substantial – especially from Norwegian clubs – started to diminish. From the clubs where I had been able to communicate the message that I was The Go-to-guy for the Balkans, the inquiries started to tick in.

This resulted in some try-outs here and there, and a few minor transfers, but nothing that yielded any real cash. Even if the market for the Balkans started to thaw, there was still some way left to go. So I needed to expand my network.

I made a simple spreadsheet in Excel, with one column for each country, and then categories according to a ranking system: *Good contact*, *Potential* and *Uncertain*. Then I entered the names of the people I knew from the various countries in the category that seemed most appropriate. The ones I had met face to face were in the category *Good contact*; others which I hadn't met, but communicated a lot with, via e-mail and phone, ended up in *Potential*. The last category was for people I had received what can almost be categorized as spam e-mails from, because they had found my contact info on FIFA's web pages. I gave highest priority to the countries where it was most important to get good contacts, based on which nationalities had already had success in Scandinavia, and which countries had a football culture similar to our Nordic one. Italy, Greece, Spain, Turkey and partly France were more or less ruled out. No one from these countries had ever made their mark in Norway, and they represented a different football culture than our own in all possible ways. Globally, I chose to include the U.S. and Australia, because the level of the players there is similar to the level in Scandinavia, as are their economic expectations.

I had hoped Per-Ove would have a lot more and better contacts internationally than what turned out to be the case. Most of his network for buying foreign players to Brann, were agents. In principle, it is a good thing to have strong agent contacts, if they should need our help to get into the Norwegian market. However, the agents Per-Ove knew, already had built their networks in Norway, so there wouldn't be any point in them working via us, since that would mean giving us half their fee. 50/50 is the standard deal between cross-border agents, and you don't get very far if you are one of those agents that wants all the cake for themselves; that usually leaves you with no cake at all. Anyway, Per-Ove had at least one solid contact in Australia who quickly came in useful. I had one good contact myself in Florida in the US, and one in Vancouver, Canada. Per-Ove was very eager to build links with Brazil, which I was a bit sceptical about. The country was flooded with agents and scouts, but also with class players, so there were opportunities there, no doubt. Per-Ove had a solid network in Norway, and still had a name there. But he was declining, and he didn't have the same demigod status outside the county limits of Bergen. Besides, I had good ins to most clubs in Norway myself, after countless phone calls, e-mails and personal meetings the year before Per-Ove got involved.

Since his network wasn't quite what I had hoped for, the most important contributions from Per-Ove were a solid, professional football knowledge and a keen eye for talent. Apart from that, he had long experience with hopeless starting points for negotiation, where he had the agility and creativity to land the deal and get a signature on a contract. Good and important skills.

The Excel sheet with our contacts was getting fuller, with various changes and additions. I expanded with categories like *Trusting, Likes black money* and indications of the current quality level of the players from each agent. In another Excel sheet, we had a summary of what sort of player material the different clubs were looking for, with one tab for each of the Scandinavian countries, and all teams in the top two divisions listed. The columns were labelled *Goalkeeper, Centre back, Left back, Right back, Midfield anchor* and so on. Far right was a column for *Budget*, and finally *Comments*. It was my job to call around to all the clubs. In most cases, I called the directors of football, but if I knew the coach well, I called the source directly. A director of football is a kind of noisy filter to an agent. His job is to relieve the pressure from the coach, filter out anything but the inquiries that seem interesting and exciting, and present a few selected cases. It happened frequently that the info about the players I introduced to the directors of football, never reached the coaches, because the director of football had bluffed and lied to me that – sure, I mentioned it to the coach, but he wasn't interested. It could be crucial to get the mobile number to the main coach, and SMS works just fine. If you manage to arouse the interest of the coach, he is the one who goes to the director of football and asks to see or buy the player you are presenting. When the director of football called me on occasions like that, they tended to be a little tense. They didn't like that I went behind their backs. But what is an agent to do? It's a well-known fact that it is not always the quality of the presented player that decides whether a director of football passes on an inquiry or not – it can be much more important who does the presenting. Everybody who makes decisions in the clubs have *their people* in the market. Therefore, sneaking and slinking, with a wink and a smile, is part of the game if you want to survive it.

Anyway, I called and called and called some more. And noted the clubs' wants and needs in the spreadsheet. Some clubs are well organized, and give very detailed and precise information about age, nationality, height, speed, left/right-leggedness, offensive/defensive, and much more. Besides, the well-organized clubs have a clear scheme for the total economy: max 60,000 for the transfer, max 50,000 in yearly wages, and max 10,000 in agent fee. These clubs were without doubt the best ones to work with, and it was a lot easier to hit with players to them. Still, and unfortunately for Norwegian football, the vast majority of our conversations went more or less like this:

– *What kind of players are you looking for ahead of the next transfer window?*

– *We are looking for a forward.*

– *All right, can you describe as precisely as possible which kind of forward you are looking for?*

– *The goal-scoring kind.*

– *Got it, Sir. And regarding the economic terms, which level are we looking at?*

– *That depends entirely on the quality of the player.*

Zero structure, and the chicken-and-egg approach when it

comes to the money. *You first – no, you first.* That gives you a hopeless starting point as agent, and you have to scan the market high and wide, and go hunting with a shotgun. Maybe do some research into which kind of football the team is playing, and assess for yourself the kind of forward they probably need. Many clubs wail about being spammed with suggestions to players from agents via e-mail and fax (!), but if they had been a little more professional themselves, and given us a detailed requirement specification to work with, they would have received much fewer, and much more precise, suggestions.

Still, the spreadsheet filled up with various wishes from clubs, and it kept changing all the time, as their needs were covered and/or new ones arose. At one point, I learned a smart trick from an agent colleague in Slovenia: – Remember to ask which players they want to get rid of! But do it discreetly; the player himself is often not aware of it.

It worked like a charm. New column far right on the spreadsheet: *Players out.* Many directors of football love you more for the players you manage to sell for them than the players you get in. Over time that tip gave us some extra cash.

In summary, we had two spreadsheets, and the information in them was golddust to an agent. To the agents I trusted, I sent the entire file. If one of the agents in my network wanted to screw me, they could contact the clubs directly and trick me out of half the fee. It happened quite a few times, and resulted in adjustments in the sheet to assure that the same asshole wasn't trusted with all the golden info over again, so he was labelled *Sneak* – in principle the same as deleting that agent for future collaboration. Over time, and with many positive and negative experiences with various foreign agents and other contacts, I built up a robust list over people we trusted more or less – who delivered the goods and who were all hat and no cattle.

I also learned the quick and painful way ALWAYS to have a copy of the agreement that gave my contact the exclusive right to represent the player I was going to sell into Norway. I was caught off guard once in Molde FK, when the player Mohamad Habib from Ghana came and signed a loan contract. The next day it was in the media, and shortly thereafter Molde FK were bombarded with e-mails and faxes from agents who claimed THEY had the exclusive contract with the player. They threatened with fines and less pleasant things. One of them even sent an invoice via fax to Molde FK, where he requested them to pay 50,000 euros to get the matter sorted out. I was super stressed and felt I had water way over my head. However, Tarje N. Jacobsen, the very experienced Director of Molde FK, reassured me that this happened quite often – it would soon quiet down. Which it did, but after this experience, I was meticulous about having everything clearly defined and in order. And the contacts who didn't accept my way of doing things, were removed from my list. All new contacts received a standard e-mail from me – here is an excerpt from it:

Dear Partner,
I have some clear philosophies in the way I work:
If I am a player's agent, I have full exclusivity in representing the player for either 6, 12 or 24 months in the countries agreed upon.
The players is the most important part, and should always be the centre of attention.
I am willing to, and very open to, involving anybody who can bring good things to the table.
If other people are involved in working for the player, I want to have full insight in what they are doing.
I give the player the exact info that I receive from clubs, even if, and especially if it is brutally hard. It is important that the player always knows what the market thinks about him.
Finally, and most important. 100% honesty and transparency between all parties involved at ALL times. Everything on the table, both good and bad.

One of these e-mails had given me the opportunity to cooperate with two agencies in Poland, and the time had come to visit them. It would turn out to be a bizarre trip, but it would also turn out to be useful to establish Polish contacts. It was a Pole who made me aware of gross corruption on the highest level in the Football Association of Norway (NFF).

POLAND TOUR

I had been in touch with the two agencies in Poland for a while before Per-Ove joined me, but so far, nothing had materialised from it, until one day, when I spoke to Trond Fylling in Sogndal Fotball, and it turned out that they were looking for a centre back. I had recently received an e-mail from Poland about the same kind of player. All the info were placed into the system I had built up, and normally e-mails like this one were thrown into folders sorted under countries, and then under the player's position on the field. But this one from Poland only contained a name, a centre back. A month earlier the same Pole had sent me another centre back, who he, needless to say, boasted of shamelessly. I placed it in the folder *Poland* without giving it a second thought. The player had been transfer free, and rumour had it German clubs were also nosing around for him. This is a classic angle for many agents, to say that large clubs in large leagues really want this player, but because of this and that and the devil and his grandmother, the transfer was cancelled at the last second. If you were to believe this, it would be incomprehensible why that same player a month later would want to play in the second highest division in Norway. It didn't make sense, and I never passed on cock-and-bull stories like this. If I had, I might just as well have put on big shoes and a clown's nose.

After a while, the player I had received info about a month earlier, turned up on the European transfer summary, which I checked a couple of times a week. He had signed for one of the minor clubs in the German Bundesliga. I made a large note to myself about this and that I would read e-mails from this Pole a little more thoroughly in the future. I fetched the e-mail about this new back. It gave a rather unconvincing explanation for why this guy would accept the Norwegian First Division, although he had played briefly for larger clubs in his youth. I called Poland to get some more details. We agreed that I should introduce him to Sogndal and suggest that he could come for a try-out about a week later. Sogndal took the bait, and the player, Lukasz Nadolski, came. He did his things well, and after a short time, he signed a 3-year contract, while our small agent company could share a substantial agent fee with the Poles. The fact that we arranged try-out and contract for their player, made the Poles very eager to get to know us better. The next week I decided to take a trip to Poland, to meet with them personally and form stronger connections.

A good friend of mine, Daniel, became enthusiastic when I mentioned in a conversation that I was going to Poland. Could he join me? – Sure, I said, – But we'll go by car, and you will have to sleep on an extra bed in my room, because Per-Ove will never agree to spend company money on a plane ticket for one of my drinking buddies. The drive would mean a few extra days out of office, but it didn't really matter that much; as long as I had my laptop, mobile phone and charger, I was fully operative.

This was going to be a road trip, including both business *and* pleasure. I love being with Daniel; we are like peas in a pod. He's the perfect travel companion to prevent cabin fever – which I usually suffered from when travelling alone to cheap hotels.

We drove via Oslo and Gothenburg before crossing the waters in a flimsy car ferry from Ystad, Sweden to Sassnitz, Germany, only a few hours' drive from the Polish border. We had agreed to meet the Poles in Stettin, right across the border. Our plan was to arrive in the city on a Friday, find a hotel, and take a look around. On Saturday, I was scheduled to meet with the Poles, and possibly see a training match with the city's home team, with the wonderful name of Morski Klub Sportowy Pogon Szczecin. I assumed the home supporters used an abbreviation or acronym; if not, I couldn't wait to hear the chants on their terraces!

We arrived to the city early in the afternoon, which seemed a classic Eastern bloc place – grey and depressing. The standard of our hotel room was very good, considering the price, but it was small, even for a single room. Daniel was, as promised, allocated a folding bed of the cheapest kind, with a mattress that looked like it was made of some kind of thick woollen material. We unfolded it out and placed it against the window on the opposite side of my bed. That left us with exactly one metre of space between us. Well, we weren't here to sleep anyway, although that is the first thing we did. It had been a long trip from Bergen, and we needed a couple of good hours' rest to get any fun out of the night. After some sleeping, showering and sharing of Polish vodka, we were ready for the city. We asked the woman on reception if she could recommend a place with good food and a nightclub for later. She was happy to, but she recommended we hire two helpers for the night instead. We didn't get it, so she had to explain.

It turned out that this city wasn't winning any prizes for low crime rates, so it was risky for foreigners to walk around by themselves after nightfall. This had created a niche for a new minor business: Helpers. You paid one or two local guys to drive you to the right places, help you pass the queues and, most importantly, make sure you stay clear of con artists and troublemakers. It sounded both weird and expensive, but the receptionist denied that. She had two friends who did this for a living, she said, and they were free tonight. We could rent them both for around fifty Polish zloty, roughly the same as the price of a pint of beer in a pub in Norway. A no-brainer. The guys came and picked us up after half an hour of refilling in the reception hall bar. They were really likeable fellows – big and bloody frightening looking, yes, but likeable. First, they took us to a steak house on the outskirts of downtown. They had called in advance, so the table was ready, already set with the Polish starters our guys had recommended on many small plates. The restaurant had a separate section for *helpers*, and our guys joined some colleagues in a sofa behind a folding screen, with a noisy TV as pastime. One of them was sitting so that he could just turn to see us, and he did so regularly. We felt like little Don Corleones with wise guys making sure a rival family didn't shoot us. The wine of the house came in two litre carafes, and it flowed incredibly fast. We saw the bottom of two carafes before deciding that it was time to move on into the night. Our guys gave us several options to choose between. Did we want a large dance floor and techno, velvety lounges with ladies in elegant dresses, or tacky disco with dancing on the tables and the naughtiest ladies in town? Option three, please. There was a long queue outside the disco, infinitely long. It went around the corner, and reminded me of the queues to the opening night tickets of The Lord of The Rings movies. Minus the adult halfwits in weird costumes.

Now our guys really gave us value for the money. First we went straight past the queue, and we didn't pay a cent to get in. Inside it was packed, and all the tables were long gone, with eight to ten chairs around tables meant for four people. Our men asked us where we wanted to sit down. We didn't quite understand the question, and mumbled something in reply in the loud music. One of them seemed to have taken Mumbling as optional subject at school, for he nodded with raised eyebrows in reply, confirming that he understood precisely what we said. Then he went over to the table closest to the dance floor – the best table for eyeing the ladies – which had twelve chairs with Polish scoundrels crowded around it. Our man asked them to gather their heads in a circle so they could hear him. He nodded; they nodded. Then he turned and pointed in our direction, smiling. Around him, twelve pair of eyes full of hate stared in the same direction. They got up, slowly and reluctantly, and disappeared into the crowd.

Light-footed, in a way that reminded me of James in *Dinner for One* when he runs to fetch the soup, our helper came smiling towards us, escorted us over to the table, and almost pushed us down on the two foremost chairs, so our toes were just touching the border to the gold-coloured tiled dance floor. – Close to the action, he said. This time they didn't go behind any folding screen to watch Polish soap; instead they sat down on the other side of our table. So we had excellent view of the long-legged, short-skirted and flirtatious Polish babes, while our fifty zloty literally covered our backs. We were already so drunk that the feeling of embarrassment we would normally have experienced from stealing someone else's table, didn't even get a look-in in our brains' management; it was more like a Polish National Assembly in there. And it seems Daniel lets loose faster than I do; he was in full party mode on the dance floor, on the scene, at the tables, at the bar. And pushing the limits of what 50 zloty could protect us from. He even poured a newly bought pint of beer over the head of a big lump of a man in singlet with fur on his back – the ape's own pint, nothing less. But our money was still good, nema problema.

Serving hours and closing times aren't as important in Poland as back home, so when it was still packed with no sign of calming down at four in the morning, I started to look for my towel; it needed to be thrown in. I was supposed to meet the Poles for lunch at 12:30 the next day. After all, this was supposed to be work, and I wanted to make a good first impression – as is well known you only get one chance at that. Therefore, I wanted to have the dryness in my mouth, the thumping in my head and the bags under my eyes more or less under control before I met them. Daniel had a Polish *pizda* wearing a super tight dress in his arms, and wouldn't hear of retreating. Our guys found the simplest solution to this mathematical problem. They were two, we were two. One stayed, one went with me. So we went back to the hotel. I got undressed, but for reasons unknown, I woke up a few minutes before the alarm call I had ordered for 11 o'clock, with my suit jacket on, naked underneath. That eerie feeling when you thought you remembered everything that happened yesterday, but clearly you don't. Up in sitting position, leaning forward. Daniel's empty and made bed switched my focus. He didn't come back last night. Missing in action. Not the first time. His mobile went straight to the answering machine. I couldn't do much more, other than hope for the best.

Daniel is an alley cat like me, and we always land on the ground, although not always on our feet. I had to take a shower, change suit, get my hair back in a slick style with moisturizer (try it) and get my agent mask on. A year earlier, I had bought a wicked leather briefcase at hundreds of euros. I bent it and greased it regularly to make it look worn. The only thing I had in it now was a packet of Orbit, where the aluminium foil had started to disintegrate and dull pieces of gum protruded from both ends, plus a few old boarding cards. Empty, that is. Nevertheless, it was destined to join me in the meeting with the Poles. Part of my look.

The meeting went quite smoothly. They were business people, not the laughter-and-shoulder-clapping kind. With their own stationary – fancy. But much cheaper briefcases. The two I met with were both right hand men to the powerful boss in one of Poland's largest agent companies. We sat for a couple of hours talking, dry and boring. We didn't have a very good chemistry, and I was a bit below par after the night before. There was also an elephant in the room that we hesitated to approach. They owed me money for some plane tickets I had prepaid for a couple of their players. And not an insignificant amount, but they had been very reluctant to pay it via bank transfer to my company account in Norway. They would rather pay me in cash in Poland. The reason they gave was that if the money was paid officially to me via a bank, it had to be registered in their systems and be subject to taxes in Poland. And they didn't want to pay taxes of money that I had to pay taxes for in Norway anyway. Their explanation didn't make any kind of sense, but the owner of this agent company was a guy you wouldn't mess around with, so even if I had my doubts, I agreed to receive the money in cash.

I took a deep breath and asked for the money. In response, I got two pairs raised eyebrows.

The second in command told me that there had been a slight change of plans. The boss himself didn't believe that I would report this amount to the authorities when I got back to Norway, thus evading the tax. Therefore, in the logic of his world, the Polish agent equivalent of Lucky Luciano would keep the share of the money that I was supposed to pay in taxes in Norway. And he knew the tax in Norway was high, so he figured fifty percent was a reasonable share. True, we do have a rigid taxation system in Norway, but I don't usually report expenses for plane tickets as taxable income. However, the case was closed from their side, and my 6000 euros were cut in half. Pure and unmitigated fraud. As if that weren't enough, they reeled off an anecdote that beat even my funny stories with a wide margin, about one thing and another that had the unfortunate result that they hadn't even brought the lousy, hair-cut three thousand euros with them. If I could return to Poland the next week?

As my daughter, Julie, would have put it: *Yeah, right!* You owe me, Jarek!

Since the football match we were supposed to watch together, didn't start until around five, and it wasn't more than two now, we quickly agreed to skip it. They seemed as happy about that as I was. Handshakes and goodbyes. Now followed by the classic, *my friend.* This term surfaces at different points from country to country, and from person to person; but agents, particularly in the eastern parts of Europe, become *friends* lightning fast, and that is fine only if there's a *good* in front of it. In that light, I have tons of good friends around Europe. And in Africa, of course, where they often open with the phrase the first time they call you. In my head, the concept of friend is a bit different, and especially someone I describe as a very good friend. And friends look after each other, so now I needed to get over to the hotel. A last wave to the Poles as they were descending an escalator in the other end of the shopping mall where we had met for lunch. A year later I got to know their boss even better. He was definitely one of the most sinister and scary people I met in my time as agent. You could tell he didn't make empty threats. Besides, he was unstable and unpredictable. Per-Ove and I decided to write off the entire amount he owed us. It simply wasn't worth the risk. I have many weak points, but I am rarely frightened, very rarely. I guess it's a sixth sense left over from ancient times. You just know it when you are clearly overpowered. I know many Polish players who would piss their pants only from hearing this guy's name.

Mission *Find Daniel* resolved quickly, as I stumbled over clothes and shoes he had stepped out as he got home. The man himself was in foetal position on his scrawny bed. He was half-awake and moaned silently. I asked the fool why he hadn't gone to sleep in my, in contrast to his, luxury queen sized one. He turned slowly, like a rheumatic old man, and whispered something. I didn't listen, since all my attention was directed at hundreds of thin scratch marks all over his upper body and face.

– *What the hell happened?*

– *Knut ...,* he said hoarsely, – *you know that crazy cat lady in The Simpsons, right?*

I confirmed; we both love Homer and his crew.

– *I went back to her place. It got nice and cosy. But there were fucking cats everywhere, man. They attacked me in packs, Knut. Must have been around twenty of them. I'm not kidding.*

I was already with my hands on my knees, close to dying of laughter. Classic Daniel.

He grinned a little in the corner of his mouth, below the hand that held his nose in a tight grip.

– *What's with your nose, Daniel?*

– *One of the motherfucking cats, a fat beast, bit me in the nose. And he didn't let go either. It hurts like hell.*

Heavy sigh from the camp bed. He removed his hand and revealed a meatball nose, with small scratches and some missing skin. We didn't spend more time on that, but decided we should rest a few hours, maybe see *Madagascar* on pay-tv again? I had a

single bed, but it was ninety centimetres wide, so not the narrowest model. Nevertheless, I regretted that I in a weak moment had invited my poor, wounded friend to lay beside me instead of on his springy thingy on thin legs on the floor. We both fell asleep to the sound of a singing lemur with a pineapple on his head:
– *I like to move it, move it. I like to MOVE IT.*
I woke at around eight in the evening. The sound that probably woke me up was a mixture of the running shower and the moaning of the guy underneath it. The remains of the cat woman had to go, down the drain and away with it. After a short while, he came out from the bathroom with a crisp shirt and styled hair. Daniel used other things than body lotion in his mane. The shirt covered the injuries on his torso, and the scratches were much less prominent now that the coagulated blood was washed off. But not even a Hollywood stylist would have managed to powder his nose pretty again. Still, the smile under his nose was there, and he was ready for Stettin by night, take 2. I already showered before the meeting, so all I needed was a dash of lotion in my hair, and I was ready. Our guys met us in the reception at nine, as we had agreed the day before. We didn't feel like gambling, so we had dinner at the same place as yesterday, and this time we managed to see the bottom of the third carafe as well. It was Saturday, and our helpers wanted to show us an incredible nightclub that was only open once a week – the day we all look forward to through a grey week.

Their claims about this place were not put to shame. This was the real deal!

The nightclub had all the elements you could want, and after a while, we were very comfortable in a deep sofa, with champagne in our glasses and a tart on each lap. Long story short, we let our hair down. We were both well off, and it was almost dead certain that we would get laid tonight. My *kurva* for the night whispered in my ear that she wanted to leave. Guys who know each other well, only need a nod and a wink to communicate in a situation like this, and we were soon outside: the *kurva*, yours truly and my half of our two helpers. He talked to her in the car, and we went a bit outside the city core, where there were street up and street down with the same depressing blocks of flats everywhere. She signalled that we were there. Drunk as a skunk I didn't realize she had played me until I got the door slammed in my face as I was about to follow her. I opened the window, asking and pleading, but she replied that she lived with her mom and dad, so the fun ended here at the pavement. Ditched by a kurva. Sweet. Not.

That night I hung my suit jacket in the closet before I went to bed, just to be sure, so my body was free from fabrics when I slid under the cover. Nice.

I woke up with a jerk, and got up almost on my knees in the bed. Straight from dreaming to knee-standing. What the fuck?!

I didn't get a second to think before someone slammed hard and intensely on my door. It felt like it was about to be smashed right in. The knocking continued, hard, mixed with loud yelling, *"Open the door, open the door, open the door."* I was completely bewildered, and like a soldier acting out an order without thinking, I whipped my legs over the edge of the bed to get to the door. *"You have to open the door,"* the voice in my head told me. SPLASH!! As my feet hit the floor, or what I expected would be the floor, I felt I was standing in water, up to well over my ankles. Absurd! I got up, and saw the room completely flooded; 15–20 centimetres of water everywhere, with small ripples from the waves my feet made. My clothes were floating around; my trousers were trying to free themselves from one of the bed legs. Instead of waiting to see if it succeeded, I remembered that I had to *open the door.* The knocking and yelling continued. I waded over the floor to the door, and twisted the lock around. That was all I needed to do; the door opened by itself. Outside were a crowd of four people; an odd lot: a thin, suited hotel employee, a security guard; a chambermaid in front of a grotesque looking machine, and finally a fireman all geared up, with a yellow hatchet in one hand. I realized that the last strand of hope I had that this might be a dream, could be abandoned. The suited one took a step ninety degrees out in the hallway, to make a hole. He pulled my shoulder out of the room, saying *look at this*! The hallway was full of people and flooded with water. Firefighters with pumps and hoses, partly dressed guests, indifferent cleaning ladies and another suited gentleman, a little older than the one by my side, walking quickly towards my door opening. I only had a second to rejoice at the funny way he walked – the high flooding forced him to lift his feet unnaturally high for each step. Suddenly he was in my face, and every bit of him smelled of hotel manager.

– *Are you Mister Hoibraaten?!?!*

– *Yes.*

– You have to pay for this. Do you hear me! You must pay!!
I tried to take in what he was saying to me, but in the same moment I realized that I was out in the hallway stark naked. The words rolled non-stop out of the mouths of the manager, fireman, security guard and suit number two. It was difficult to process it all on top of the self-awareness my nakedness brought forth, the fact that I had been sound asleep a few moments ago, and the alcohol I had been drinking only hours earlier. The water floating around everywhere was not the ideal setting for clear, calm thinking either. Our room was on the third floor. Through the cacophony from the agitated crowd around me, I managed to get the picture after a minute or so. The entire hotel was flooded from the third floor and down, and the only room the water could come from, was ours.

Daniel likes to take a shower when he gets back from a night out, or preferably to have a bath. However, since most hotel rooms don't have a bathtub, he has gotten the bad habit of blocking the outlet in the shower with a towel, to, if possible, gather a few centimetres of water where he can relax. He did something similar in my own wedding in a hotel in Frogner, Oslo. The only damage from that incident was a ruined outlet grille. Later we read in the newspaper that a man did the same thing in a hotel in Aalesund, with the result that the entire room was flooded, and he had to pay 35,000 euros in damages. For one single room. And we had flooded an entire bloody hotel from the third floor and down. *Fuck you, Daniel!*

I took a step to the side, to verify that Daniel was indeed lying in his bed. I ignored all the yelling around me, and walked with determined, and probably comical, steps towards the one I was dead sure had caused this mess. He slept naked on top of the bed cover, exposed. With his back at us, snoring. Jesus Christ, are you deaf, man? When I was one step from him, I felt something brushing against my calf. It was a large bath towel floating past me. I bent down and grabbed one end of it. It was heavy and soaked. Many will remember how we used to slap each other using the towel as a whip after P.E. in school. At least I did at that point, and I rotated the towel up, bent back like a discus-thrower to catch momentum. A loud smack as I hit him the first time, and a wide, red streak appeared instantly over his ribs and belly. New momentum, new blow. The towel hit him again as he was turning around, awake now after the pain from the first blow. He opened one eye and saw me yelling in front of him. Then he uttered some half-drunk nonsense, before he did the same move as I had a short while back, swung his legs over the edge of the bed, and SPLASH! Both eyes wide open now. The group of fiery lemmings had followed me into the room and were standing right beside me. Except for the fireman – he was in the bathroom turning off the running shower. The lemmings had talked continuously since the moment I opened the door, and Daniel thought he had figured out who the hotel manager was. Uncertain he opened his mouth to ask, *"Are you the manager of this place?"* Confirmation. Whereupon Daniel growled loudly to the man, *"What the fuck kind of hotel is this? There's water all over the floor, man?!"*

Afterwards that was hilarious, the punch line for that day. But not when it happened. Definitely not. That was the last straw for the manager, who exploded in a mix of all the Polish and English curses he could think of. In addition to the mantra he kept repeating:

– YOU MUST PAY!

The fireman interrupted the flow of curses to inform us that the cause of the flooding was stopped. We had a discussion a few minutes that didn't make sense to any of us, given that the lemmings were in shock and furious, while we were in shock and hungover. In a moment of divine inspiration I managed to ask nicely if we could have a few minutes to get dressed, then we'd come down to the reception and continue the talking there. Thank God, they accepted our plan and left the scene of the crime. I closed the door as quickly as physically possible when you have to shove around buckets of water in the process. Click. Exhale.

At first I was the only one talking, and only scolding and bile came out of my mouth, directed at Daniel. He replied with some *but... you know... I thought... but...*

We sat down on our respective beds, calmed our hyperventilation a bit, and activated the clear thought mode many people go into in situations like this. We refreshed our memories with the episode from Aalesund, and agreed that we faced certain bankruptcy. Who could we call for help? The Embassy? We quickly dismissed that idea. We decided to call Erlend, a buddy of both of us who worked in Polygon. They do property damage restoration after fire and flooding, among other things. He would have some good advice for us. But alas, no reassuring words from him regarding the cost estimate, if we had caused serious water damages on four floors. Still, he did have one piece of advice, and it had nothing to do with his line of work. He figured the best we could do, was to take all our clothes out of our suitcases and put them on one layer over another. That way we might be able to sneak unnoticed passed the reception. Maybe. The only thing that was certain, was that we could forget about unnoticed if we brought our suitcases. *"Best of luck, guys."* Click.

We didn't have any better ideas, so we seized the advice hungrily, put on all our clothes and slipped out of the room. Thank God we had our passports in our possession. It's not at all uncommon that they are left behind in the reception for registration. But I had already paid the room with my Visa card. We sneaked along the hallway as quietly as we could, feeling a little like a couple of Beagle Boys. Right beside the elevator was a white door with a green sign above it: *Fire escape.* We looked at each other, and speed-read each other's minds. Down the escape staircase and out the back entrance, sneaked around the corner towards the driveway in front of the main entrance to find our car that was parked there. One, two, ignition, first gear, second gear. And we put metre after metre between the hotel and us; restrained rejoicings in the car. We drove straight towards the border, ridden by anxiety. After a short half hour we had talked each other so far up that our nerves were making ripples on the outside of our skin. We were convinced we were Polska's most wanted, and that they had our photos at the border crossings. After some fiddling with the map, we agreed that it would definitely be much smarter to cross the border a bit further to the north, on a cart road; they probably wouldn't have heard about us there yet. So we turned the car and found the correct exit road. Two hours later, after a few unfortunate detours, we finally spotted the border post. It was as we had imagined: two men in a shed with a corrugated roof.

Daniel's passport was approaching its expiry date; in other words, it was almost ten years old, and ten years ago Daniel had straight and blond hair down to his shoulders. He was a handsome man; some would even say a pretty man. After ten years of travelling, his passport had been through a lot, and it was issued the first year Norway introduced a new type of passport, which only lasted for a couple of years, before they made a more durable variant. Daniel's was of the old, flimsy kind. Besides it had been crumpled and curled so many times in his pockets and elsewhere, that some air had been trapped inside the plastic covering his photo, so his photo had become discoloured in some parts, including around his eyes. It looked like he was wearing mascara. So when we drove up to the man in the booth, sweating and nervous like the fugitives we were, the man wondered why Daniel was trying to get into Germany with a strange lady's passport. Daniella is a common woman's name in Poland. And who could blame the border guard? Not a single feature from his passport photo resembled the Daniel sitting in the passenger seat. Allahu Akbar for low wages in Poland. A hundred euros got Daniel across the border, and we set course for Norway and Bergen.

After a night's sleep in our own beds at home, both reason, consciousness and a dose of morals caught up with both of us. Therefore, we wrote a long e-mail to the hotel and gave our contact info. I wonder if honesty, albeit somewhat delayed, actually does pay. I could physically feel my body becoming lighter after reading the reply from the hotel manager. No problem, the insurance covered it all. You are welcome to come back. Needless to say, everyone we knew heard the story of our trip, and three other buddies spent an entire week of their vacations in the Polish city, believing that this was a place where all kinds of crazy stuff happened. A week they could just as well have Ctrl-Alt-Deleted; nothing happened, except that they got to know each other a little better.

A while later I got another good contact in Poland – a much less scary one this time. He was, like myself, relatively fresh to the game. His name is Marcin Hakman. We often called one another with football related questions – not just to push players. Once I called him for counsel in connection with a transfer to England, since he had done that earlier; I got good help. Another time he called me because he needed advice. He was about to sign a Polish goalkeeper in Sogndal, Piotr Leciejewski, and almost everything was settled; the transfer amount, player wages and agent fee was all agreed upon. But there was one obstacle left.

The way he understood things, the manager and the director of football in Sogndal Fotball wanted some money under the table to sign the player. – Okay, I said, a little surprised, but not too much. This is quite common in Europe, but less so in Norway than many other countries. The Polish agent didn't have any issues with them wanting money under the table; he was well acquainted with that from his home country. His main reason for calling me, was to ask about the normal level in Norway; he didn't want to be duped.

– *How much did they ask for?* I asked.

– *5000 euros each.*

– *Sounds fair enough,* I replied. And I meant it.

I had heard repeated rumours in the agentosphere that the director of football in Sogndal Fotball, Trond Fylling, was a sly fox. But I didn't know much about the manager. We had only talked on the phone a couple of times and exchanged a few e-mails related to the transfer of Lukasz Nadolski one year earlier.

Marcin Hackman thanked me for the counselling, and told me he would accept their demand for a total of 10,000 euros to land the deal, confident that he wasn't overpaying the management of Sogndal.

After hanging up with Marcin, I made a note to myself that Sogndal's manager was of the questionable kind. I knew many of those, but as mentioned, few in Norway. I found it almost endearing that there were tricksters in the idyllic "lemonade village" of Sogndal. Well, I didn't spend much more time thinking of that; that is, not until the same manager who, according to what I heard, had received money under the table, ran for election as president of The Football Association of Norway. And he won the election! Then I *did* think more about it – a lot actually. It sent chills down my rather cynical and tough-skinned spine: something is rotten in the state of Norway.

Yngve Hallén became President in March 2010. Almost two years later, after several alleged cases of corruption in Norwegian football were mentioned in the media, president Hallén stood up and promised that he would leave no stone unturned to fight this crap. Lawyers would be hired in to review all transfers into and out from Norway several years back. The law firm Smedsrud Stoltz AS were hired as project managers, and Smedsrud hired the law firm LYNX Advokatfirma to do the actual investigation. The report that was finally presented to the association, was given the name *The 1192 Report*, simply because there had been 1192 transfers in the period 2007–2011. A vetting process was first conducted, which left 22 transfers to be thoroughly investigated.

In the course of the investigation, which took slightly less than a year, LYNX Advokatfirma expressed their dissatisfaction with what they claimed to be difficult working conditions. LYNX approached the Football Association several times to inquire about documentation, including the bi-annual accounts all clubs are required to submit to the association to get their club license approved. The association refused to disclose this. Moreover, they were building a database with all information that was necessary and relevant to the investigation. The work with the database proceeded slowly, and it took a long time before LYNX got access to things like player contracts.

To sum it up, LYNX was refused access to possibly material and very important information in connection with their investigation, and they wrote the following in their report:

Some indications have been found that point to serious financial crime. However, there is a big difference between indications and conclusions.

In other words, LYNX are saying that they found indications that serious crimes were committed, but they can't specify this because the necessary information that could have documented any crimes, were never released by the Association.

Needless to say, the transfers to and from Sogndal during the president's time as manager in the club, were also subject to investigation. The conclusion was that the entire body of Norwegian football was acquitted and cleared of suspicions. No crime committed. And Yngve got the tension-relieving *All clear, Sir* from his platoon of lawyers.

So I made my decision. Fair enough that I use tons of private-label body lotion in my hair, and that I am smarmy and cunning if I have to. But I have grown up in a home where the trade union movement had a strong position, and learned to insist on my rights and fight the superiority. I found it difficult to pocket that Yngve slipped away, so I sent an e-mail to my friend Marcin:

Hi Marcin. Long time. Sorry we didn't meet when you were in Bergen. I hope you had a good stay in this beautiful city :-)

Already the Clubs have started looking for players for Next year. Can you send me a list of good players you recommend for 1 and 2 League in Norway? Thanks. I also have a question. Do you remember when Piotr went to Sogndal from Poland, and the sports director and director of Sogndal asked for some Money from you "under the table", and you asked me if this was normal also in Norway. Do you remember how much this was (I think you said 5000 or 15000 euro??).

All the best!
Knut   :-)

Hi Knut,
In Bergen was nice. With Piotr we went to Ulriken Mountain, it was very
hard but the view was fantastic. Bergen is really amazing city. I was also on the
game and had meeting with Sport Director. Now the season is finish, Piotr is
not happy with Brann position after the season but maybe in next season will
be better.
Please let me know for which position You will be looking players, I have a
few proposal from Poland, Bulgaria. I would like to recommend you a right
defender (national player from Bulgaria) Pavel Vidanow from Zaglebie Lubin.
His contract is till 30.06.2014 but I can take him for a small transfer fee or
even for free.
For division 1 - I have a young goalkeeper (1994) who can be like Piotr in
the future.
Knut: About Sogndal and money under the table...I hope that you don't
tell to Sogndal it was a long time ago and I don't want to make a problems.
But to you knowledge it was around 5000 euro.
I hope that we can make minimum one transfer in this season as you know
Piotr and Fojut shows that the players from Poland are good.
Best regards
Marcin

I replied that I wouldn't tell. Sorry, Marcin, for not keeping that
promise. However, believe me when I say that I am pretty sure
nobody in Sogndal will be angry with you; their anger will probably
be directed at the person who deserves it.

When I received this e-mail, I thought Sogndal had only one
"head of club", and in reality they did. However it turned out that
several people used this title when communicating in writing. After
the first edition of this book was published, the Norwegian
Confederation of Sports engaged the auditing firm BDO to launch
an investigation. BDO didn't find any basis for the allegation that
Hallén should have received any of this money. Their report stated
that several persons in Sogndal used the title "head of club" in
communication with the outside world, including Trond Fylling,
who wasn't employed by the club anymore. In addition to signing

the e-mails to the Poles as "head of club", it also turned out that Fylling had approved an invoice for payment of agent fee from Sogndal to the agent Marcin Hakman, where Fylling himself should receive a share of the money. Trond Fylling was criticised for his dual roles and disorderly conduct in connection with the transfer, but no further investigation was conducted. The president only commented that "it was a practical solution that Fylling did it like that."

I wonder if that applies in general, that it's practical to let the agent both sign the player's contract and approve the agent fee to himself. In that case there may be good times ahead for football agents.

Anyway, when The 1192 Report was published by LYNX, the online newspaper Nettavisen asked Yngve Hallén what his feelings were today, when he had the conclusion in his hands?

– I am very, very, very happy that we did this. When we started out, I had a bad gut feel about whether this was the right thing to do.

I wonder why …

We live in a state governed by law, where we are innocent until proven guilty. I don't really know if the money Macin mentioned in his e-mail were ever paid out, neither do I know which of the "managers" he was referring to.

THE GOLD'S COMING HOME

Holding my newly tuned sitar in my hands;
all my grief left me on the peak of Ulriken.
Thought of the beacons if they would be lighted,
and against foes order out the marching men.
Felt the calm upon me, rejoiced in my spirit,
and reached for my sitar with playful hands.
— "Views from Ulriken" ("Udsikter fra Ulriken") – the town song of Bergen

Brann Stadion, October 28, 2007, at 6:59 p.m. The entire crowd on a packed stadium, 18,200 patriotic Brann supporters, singing the city's "national anthem" with their hearts on the outside of their parkas in the chilly autumn weather. Brann was playing home against Viking Stavanger. Normally an exciting local Western Norway derby in itself, but this evening something far, far bigger. Tonight it could all be decided. The air under the floodlights was electric, and the setting couldn't have been better. As the referee's whistle, drowned out by the crown, started the battle, the stadium classic song, which over the years had collected an increasingly heavy burden of irony, resounded from the crowd:

We're the famous Brann from Bergen, champions of the league this year.
Bloody hell, that's what we'll be, like in 1963,
while we laugh at all the peasants of our land.

135

This song felt increasingly awkward for each year that passed since 1963. But this evening, the warriors in red on the field put all irony aside, and went out with all muscles and joints fully prepared for battle against Stavanger's proud blue men.

We had the opportunity to settle it all the week before, away against Aalesund. Many Brann supporters went to the Art Nouveau city to experience live the first league championship since 1963. In addition to the tens of thousands gathered before a large outdoors screen in downtown Bergen, not to mention all those watching from the comfort of their sofas. All living and crawling things between the seven mountains of Bergen had only one focus that night: Gold and redeemed honour!

Unfortunately, the match had a crappy ending, Huseklepp incredibly managed to put the ball on the inside of the left post, whereupon it traced the goal line, hit the right post and went out. If Huseboy had remembered to cut his toenails before the match, it would probably have been a goal. However, when the huge disappointment after the match lightened, there was a general agreement that there had to be a higher meaning to this. Now we had the opportunity to become champions home against Viking in the next match. All the ingredients were right for a magic night for the history books.

Per-Ove and I had permanent places in the VIP lounge, with a table for four in the restaurant, right beside the window and a door out to the seats outside. Because of Per-Ove's status in Brann, we got these places at a good price. Several locals had probably paid thousands of euros to be able to sit here to watch the match against Viking in the autumn of 07. We often brought players, agents, scouts or club representatives to Brann Stadion, as was common in our business, if someone wanted to watch a particular player on the field, of course, but also as an arena for relaxed business talk and male bonding. If we didn't have any business arrangements for a match, we had an agreement that Per-Ove and I could freely use two of the seats as we wished. So all my friends had spent the week since Huseklepp's miss in Aalesund buttering me up in hopes of becoming my *plus one* for the Viking match. However, promises of one year's car wash, a trip to Vettismorki in the Jotunheimen mountains (as if that was a prize worth having!) or free booze, made no difference. I had, unfortunately, months ago and without thinking about how important this match might become, promised a scout from the Turkish club Trabzonspor a place at the table in connection with a Norway tour he was taking the last week of October. That sucked, of course, but a promise was a promise, and Trabzonspor is a large club and potentially good client. That's why my *plus one* on the greatest day in Bergen the last fifty years, was a middle-aged Turk who spoke bad English. Per-Ove, on the other hand, let it slide that evening, and was already well down into the glasses with a friend when the Turk and I arrived at the table an hour before the match started. I was dressed in an Italian tailor-made suit, with a Bosnian cashmere coat to keep out the autumn chill.

We had a nice time around the table the hour before the match started, with good food and drink. The general atmosphere in the premises was exceptional. Out on the grandstand even the Turk, who was used to enthusiastic crowds, was visibly impressed with the atmosphere. The match in itself wasn't exciting; Viking was completely overrun by Brann. Brann's superiority meant that the crowd saw at an early stage which way this was going. For an old fox like myself, with the close and personal relationship I had to Brann, it was an unforgettable evening. I tried my best to stay more or less low-key, out of respect for my company, but when ten minutes remained of the match, the entire crowd got up. Old and young, rich and poor, assholes and nice folks; we all sang, in perfect sync and harmony, the song – to the tune of the old folk song used in *Sloop John B* by The Beach Boys, *I Wanna Go Home* by Johnny Cash, and by FC United of Manchester, to mention a few – that had become a mega hit among the crowds on Brann Stadion and in Bergen that year:

From Nymark to Laksevåg
From Nordnes to Loddefjord Torg
All of Bergen know the gold's coming home
The gold's coming home
The gold's coming hooooome
Home to Bergen
The gold's coming home

It was sung on repeat towards the end, and it was awesome! I looked at all my brothers around me. During my whole life as a football supporter, this had been a distant dream the people of

Bergen had almost stopped believing in. I couldn't care less about the Turk, and joined in the singing with all my heart. Shivers. I thought proudly that I had given my small, but direct, contribution to what was happening out there on the field.

Then the tears came. There I was, big, tough FIFA-licensed agent in a cashmere coat, sobbing. To the extent that football can be called a religion, my sect and I were one in that moment. Screw old, false clichés. I love my daughter more than anything in this world. But this evening on Brann Stadion, this entire experience, was a much, much greater moment than when she was born.

This night was also my definite peak as agent. Our company was growing quickly, and we were heading for the stars.

Luckily I had no idea about the brutal downturn that lay ahead of me

YOU TOO CAN BECOME AN AGENT

I am assuming that you, the reader of this book, like football. At least here, in this chapter. You like football, and so countless times have torn your hair out over stupid tactical choices that coaches have made, incomprehensible substitutions, not to mention hopeless player acquisitions. You whine and complain, to your loved one, to friends and to colleagues. And from the ones who get tired of listening to it, or simply aren't very interested in the subject, you may have heard something like, "Do it yourself then, if you think you are so much better at it!"

That usually ends the discussion. You are reminded that after all, you are just a mortal, beer-drinking coach potato, and not one of those appearing on TV every Sunday, wearing sweat suits with logos on both trousers and jackets, giving rational explanations for both victories and losses.

Listen to me, papa Doc: That is wrong! You, sitting on your sofa with crisps in your lap; you *can* do it better than the guys who get TV time. At least most of you can. It's a giant misconception that a good football player is also going to be good at spotting talent, or a good director of football or coach. Many clubs have a strange tradition of hiring retired players as coach, director of football, manager and even marketing director. These are companies – which is what a football club is, from first division and up, with budgets of up to hundreds millions of euros – who hire people in very central and demanding positions, people who often haven't spent even a single hour in a classroom after

139

compulsory schooling and who have no work experience whatsoever. They have been good football players, often at the expense of things the rest of us have had to struggle through. "*He scored more than a hundred goals for the club in his career, it's obvious that he is going to be a good director of football!*" If I had been an investor in that club, I would have yelled, "*Hell no!*"

The one reasonable thing, which almost all clubs in the world – and two in Norway – have figured out, is the importance of hiring skilled talent scouts. The two Norwegian clubs who did this, are Rosenborg and Molde, with Stig Torbjørnsen in Rosenborg and John Vik in Molde (now Cardiff), respectively. Aalesund have come into line to a degree with Harald Aabrekk. Rosenborg and Molde have seen the light, and now they are insisting on keeping this arrangement, because it gives them a clear athletic and economic advantage. Among the many serious problems in Norwegian football, this may be the most serious of them, that 95 percent of Norwegian clubs don't have a clue when it comes to efficient and accurate player logistics.

No wonder one club after another is on the verge of bankruptcy. I can guarantee that there are many, many football supporters everywhere who are very successful in some company, because they are really good at what they are doing, who would have accepted minimum wages to do the same job in the club of their hearts, bringing in their skills, knowledge and passion. To the clubs who get this, I have only one thing to say, "*Congratulations!*"

And again, to you who are in despair over a bad player purchase you club has done; yet another player who flops; yet another bad excuse. You who tear your hair out over all the clueless acquisitions, if you only knew about all the mind-blowing opportunities your club has rejected. I have a number, an alarming number, of examples of this, but I am going to tell you about only two of them:

One of my contacts abroad, who I knew I could trust when he recommended a player, came to me with a good goalie. This contact hates the traditional boasting games agents play, and he hates giving guarantees about a player's quality. However, with this goalkeeper he was so sure about his case that he was willing to put his good name and reputation on the line. He told me straight out that "*this goalkeeper, Knut, is going to be goalkeeper on the national team. I can guarantee it!*"

These were very strong words coming from my contact; but I trusted him. He had a career behind him as goalkeeper himself, for Liverpool FC.

So, dear supporters of all Tippeliga clubs in Norway. Every single one of your clubs had repeated possibilities through an entire year to have this player trying out for free, no strings attached. And they all said no, repeatedly. I had almost given up when I managed almost to force him onto a plane to La Manga. It happened on a few hours' notice, and they didn't really want him there at all, but they were tired of my nagging. The name of the boy I desperately tried to sell over the course of an entire year, was Anders Lindegaard, and he is the greatest goalkeeping success in Norway ever, both in terms of football playing and economics.

I like the second example even better, because the tip came from an artisan – my father in law's best friend. My father in law and Michael have dedicated seats on Brann Stadion, with their names on them, for which they have paid 2000 euros each. Not because they think it's cool to have their names on the seats, but because they love Brann. My parents-in-law live only a couple of hundred metres from the arena, and he and Michael are present on every single home match. Always.

To give kudos to the supporters who have actually used their annual ticket the way it's meant to be used, and dragged their butts to the arena, every club with any self-respect should play the song by The Who – *Won't Get Fooled Again* after the number of spectators are being published. Come on, NFF! Somebody have to stick their head in the loo and smell the crap. We all know that Sepp Blatter gets away with mostly anything, but we're not blind! If there are 4000 people on the arena, there are 4000 people there. NOT 9800, which is the number of tickets you sold. And please drop the silly excuse that it has to do with the VAT accounting! Don't you have basic knowledge of economics? Oh, right, you were playing football while the rest of us went to school. But NFF cannot use that excuse. I call bullshit!

My father-in-law and Michael are always among those who are counted in the real number of spectators. It weighs heavy on my patriotic heart to take in that many of my fellow citizens don't use their annual ticket. They don't show up when Brann is doing poorly. Well, actually, I do understand you; to be honest I don't either. That is why it's so special that my father-in-law and Michael have attended to every single match for 30 years, because father-in-law is from Sortland far north in Norway, and Michael is from Denmark.

Anyway, Michael tipped me off about a Danish forward, Niclas Pedersen, who he thought looked exciting. I checked him in my system, and contacted his agent. Sure, this was a talented guy, but he needed a new environment. If I could get Brann to agree to let him try there for a year, they could get him without any transfer fee. I did a little research about the player, and he seemed very promising. So I called Brann. They weren't interested – after all, they would have to pay his salary. Good point.

Another phone call to Denmark. The boy made pretty good money there, but he was so hungry to play that he would agree to an annual salary of 35,000 euros. I started to like his spirit as well, and I got an idea. I suggested to Per-Ove that we could tell Brann we would cover his wages for a year, and then get half of any transfer fee. Per-Ove watched clips of the player, saw that he was good, and agreed to the plan. And when I called Brann to present it, I was one hundred percent sure they would say yes. However, they declined. Two days later the transfer window closed, but luckily the boy managed to slip into another Danish club just in time. Three months later, he was sold for 2 million euros. Say no more. You wouldn't have made the worst director of football, Michael.

A friend of mine, Christoffer Ringdal, has a great interest in football. And there are many like him. A few years back he called me about a local young lad he wanted me to have a look at. The player's mother was one of Christoffer's co-workers, and he told her he knew an agent – me. He asked me if I could have a chat with the player and his mother. I told Christoffer I would call him back with a reply the next day. It is of course not uncommon for parents to have an elevated opinion of their children, so I was familiar with these kind of chats. Still, I wanted to hear Kjetil's and Per-Ove's opinions first. Kjetil, who was responsible for the talent development in Brann, knew all the talents in the region by heart; and Per-Ove too had a good overview. Sure, they knew the name, but he wasn't close to becoming a real football player. So I politely declined, and forgot about this guy. Today, however, I know very well who Bård Finne is.

So to get back to my point: You, back home on your coach,

know just as much about football as the people with the fat wallets. It's just in their interest to keep that a secret. Because if you're just as good as them at spotting talent, and on top of that you have five years' education and ten years' of job experience, who would the investor prefer to hire – capiche?

Alternatively, you can become an agent, but for God's sake do not take that pesky agent exam to become a licensed agent. Stay clear of that lot. I got an eye-opener in my second year as licensed agent. There was some messy business around Morgan Andersen, and I happened to be on the outskirts of it. The thing was that Morgan, at that time manager of Fredrikstad FK, hadn't submitted documentation to the association about the fact that I should receive 60,000 euros in connection with Ardian Gashi's transfer to the club. He should have done that, of course, but all major parties – tax authorities and so on – were informed. So both invoicing, payment and accounting were done cleanly on both sides. Nevertheless, The Football Association of Norway (NFF) threatened me with sky-high fines for violation of the FIFA regulations. Luckily, they withdrew their allegations after a short time, but it was a frightening experience, because the violations they accused me of, were nowhere near breaking any applicable laws – only the ones FIFA had made for themselves.

Still, I wasn't able to get angry with Morgan A. He is more the kind of guy who wakes your paternal instinct. But because I had a license issued by FIFA, and had signed a statement confirming that I would follow their rules, I had placed myself in Sepp Blatter's claws. Wide-eye-opener. While keeping as still as I could on the sideline, I stopped paying the license to the association and cancelled my agent insurance. If they should accuse me of something I didn't do at a later point in time, I would be protected by the law. I also had to pay a ridiculously high fee to the football association each year, buy an expensive insurance and cope with a red tape regime made in hell. I am no longer the only one with that opinion; at the FIFA Congress in May 2013, they decided to phase out the system of licensing football agents. Apparently, the reason was to create more transparency around transactions and the people who are involved in transfers. The decision has not come into force yet, but within not too long, licensed agents will become part of history. Who let the dogs out? Woof woof!

To sum it up, here is my advice if you want to become an agent:

Stick to the law, not to Sepp Blatter's corrupt fat fingers. You have all the right in the world to contact any player and any club. Just make sure you play clean and pay your taxes; that way you ensure that neither you nor the club or the player do anything illegal. And don't let any association make you believe otherwise, because that is bullshit!

Thus I say, raise up from the crisp crumbs on your sofas, my football brethren. Pick up your phone and call them, attend to trainings and talk to them. Give it all the knowledge and passion I know you have. You ARE just as good as they are. BELIEVE ME!

JERRY MAGUIRE

If you measure an agent's success in terms of money, I have to be honest and say that I am way down on that list, compared to most of my colleagues in Norway.

If you are a player who reads this book, I would like to recommend a handful of agents:

Morten Wivestad is a clever and smart agent. He is behind many large and very impressive transfers into and out of Norway. But he is not of the kind who likes to brag to the media. I remember when Per-Ove and I had breakfast in his house at the time when Vadim Demidov's father had put a price on his head in connection with his son's transfer from Hønefoss to Rosenborg. In the newspaper VG, you could read that Vadim's father, Sergei, had hired the mercenary slash celebrity goon Espen Lie to get the money he claimed he was entitled to. Morten was really, really scared. I think we all would have been.

Another one is Petter Bø Tosterud. He is simply very good at what he does – probably the best agent in Norway from a professional point of view. He and his father purchased the rights to FC Lyn's player squad when they went bankrupt. That gave them the opportunity to manage the sales and resale rights of the squad, and they made some money on that. He was looking for an established football agent as a joint venture partner, so he contacted several of his colleagues, including me. We had a nice lunch on Pastasentralen in Bergen, next door to the Football Pub. I perceived it as a sort of interview, since Petter knew he had lots of goodies to offer. A few weeks later, he made his choice, and said he wanted to cooperate with me. It was a flattering offer, but unfortunately, it didn't amount to anything in the end.

Tore Pedersen does a very good job for his players. He has experienced people inventing rumours to hurt him, but risen above it. Pedersen is a safe choice. He is also well liked by the decision-makers in the clubs, and that is a very important and positive thing.

It is said that the Eskimo have hundred words for snow, although I have also heard that they don't in reality, but they do know a lot about the various facets and nuances of snow after generations of living in the icy north. I consider myself about a quarter Albanian, after having lived there several years in all. And on the Balkans, we have at least hundred words for mafia. One of these describes the trio Jim Solbakken, Eirik Bakke and Ole Gunnar Solskjær very precisely. Unfortunately the English language doesn't have the appropriate word, and we Western Europeans tend to be far too gullible.

My *own private* impression of Jim is that he is a man suffering from grandiose delusions. I don't know either Jim nor Ole Gunnar personally, but the impression I have after years of watching and listening to them in the media, plus input from other agents, coaches and club leaders, is one of two completely different personality types. That is why I find it a bit difficult to believe that they have been best friends for years.

Ole Gunnar appears to be open, honest, humble, caring, down-to-earth and warm, while Jim seems to be the complete opposite: closed, aloof, cold, manipulating and very arrogant. Something is not right. My theory is that Ole Gunnar in reality either has the same personality as Jim, or that he is a victim in the firm grip of a manipulating bastard. A bold claim, yes, but think for yourself – most of us (if you are not a psychopath yourself) have one time or another found themselves in the web of a manipulator – either a girlfriend, boyfriend, friend, colleague or school friend. Despite his demigod status as football player, Ole Gunnar is just an ordinary guy from Northwestern Norway. After his career started to take off, he was probably screwed over several times by people with *apparently good intentions.* It's a classic situation that celebrities attract all the scum and parasites of the earth. After a while, you get a thicker skin and become more sceptical to whom you can trust and which agenda people have. Is it me they like, or my money and status? In those cases, it feels safer to fall back on the people you knew before becoming a celebrity; you know you can trust them and that they like you for the person you are.

Maybe this didn't work out very well in Ole Gunnar's case; maybe he bet on the wrong horse from his childhood. I am just guessing here; I may be completely wrong, or I may have a point. However, the fact remains that there has been a mix-up of their roles, as described earlier in this book.

Last, but definitely not least, I want to mention the agent Stig Lillejord. He is good – don't get me wrong – but he spreads himself too thin. He is from Bergen, and he is probably the biggest agent in Norway in terms of the number of transfers, not to mention the number of players he has represented – several hundreds of them. We live in the same city, but bizarrely we never met. He has done a lot of great stuff and made a lot of money; worked hard. And many players have been pissed off at him because he never had time for them. However, he is only human, and I know how difficult players can be. At our peak, Per-Ove and I had fifty players in our portfolio, and it was a complete chaos. At the same time, Stig had over 150. He had roughly four to eight players in each club in the topmost Norwegian division – Tippeligaen – and he used them as leverage in negotiations. If one of them didn't get a better contract, he would advise the other ones to change club. Several clubs hated him for this, but they had no choice but to play by his rules.

Even if I consider myself Mr. Nobody economically speaking, my life as agent was fabulous most of the time. I had decent pay, and I was on exciting trips 200 days a year – trips that gave me some incredible experiences. Moreover, money cannot compare with the joy it gives you to fix a good contract for a player; seeing how happy you make his family – for it can be a dog's life to be a football player. They are constantly measured and assessed, and it is impossible to make long-term plans. If you, towards the end of a contract, are injured in a way the Germans describe as *karriereende* (career ending), then you are really fucked, and your next appointment will more than a little likely be with your local public welfare office. Players are under constant pressure, and many of them struggle with jittery nerves and low self-esteem. A special job in those cases is to sit through long nights and talk them up again. I had that kind of relationship with several of my players, and especially one; he called me Jerry Maguire.

The south coast boy Kenneth Udjus had a permanent seat on the bench in Brann, and struggled with his self-esteem, as anyone would in that situation. He was at rock bottom. I used to make pasta, and together we made plans for the next week, next month, three months, six months, twelve months; and finally dream target. His dream target was playing on the national team and on an English club team.

The short-term plan was to get his confidence up where it belonged. Expose himself in training; stop seeing himself as the second goalkeeper; put up a real fight for a place on the team; pep talk himself every single day. He used to call me both before and after training – or I called him. There was real progress. After some time I managed to arrange a swap agreement between Brann and Sogndal. Neither of the clubs were interested initially, but after a lot of hard work, I managed to carry it off. Sort of. Reaching an agreement for Kenneth Udjus' new salary in Sogndal went smoothly; same thing with Piotr, the goalkeeper going over to Brann. The hindrance that delayed the process for months, was the last one of the trio, Cato Hansen. His agent refused to accept the salary Sogndal offered. According to his agent, Cato was a player of international class, and far better than both Kenneth and Piotr. After a ridiculously long process, the parties finally reached the conclusion that Brann got Sogndal's goalkeeper, Leciejewski, and Sogndal got Kenneth Udjus and the forward Cato Hansen. There was a big difference between what Kenneth made in Brann and what Sogndal could offer. Kenneth had just bought a new flat, and needed to be able to service his mortgage. I ended up paying the difference – a substantial amount for me.

Today Piotr is considered one of the best goalkeepers in Norway, and Kenneth became hugely successful and received an offer from England. Cato Hansen, who according to his agent was one of Norway's top players, doesn't play for anyone today, after having wandered from club to club downwards in the system, and he still hasn't scored a single goal!

It was pure joy to watch Kenneth flourish as first goalkeeper for Sogndal. He did very well indeed, and we often talked – about the Pop Idol celebrity Tone Damli for instance. I will never forget the day he called me as I was walking from the terminal building on Bergen Airport Flesland to pick up my car. He screamed into the phone, "Jerry, they called me from the national A-team. I may be selected!"

Please bear with me, but it was as if taken straight out of the movie with the same name he had given me. Touching.

Next goal for Kenneth was to play for his home team IK Start in Kristiansand. I had worked on them regularly during the last year, and finally they yielded. They wanted to offer him a contract. This was a few months after the movie moment, and I called Kenneth to give him the great news. He was on vacations in the U.S. and said he would call me when he got back home. However, he wasn't so sure about IK Start anymore. I was baffled. There had been something funny in his voice, so I texted him the next day. No reply. Until three days later, when he sent me a long and dramatic message about how depressed he was, and that he had decided to quit his entire football career. He thanked me for everything, and finished by saying that he would call me when he got home.

I became extremely worried, but I had to do my job and inform IK Start, so they could look for another goalkeeper. I just told them he was quitting football. They too regretted it, but they didn't dig any further. A few days later, I was completely stunned; the same man from IK Start called me, storming and raging, calling me a damned piece of crap and liar of the worst kind. What for? Well, the man from IK Start had heard from very reliable sources that Kenneth was going to sign for Lillestrøm, with Tore Pedersen as agent.

I had been agent for long enough not to start crying on my mom's shoulder when something like this happened. But angry? You bet I was! The first thing I did was forwarding the messages Kenneth had sent me, to make sure IK Start understood that he had duped me too. Then I tried to get hold of the sneak himself; that wasn't easy. The next day, as a lightning bolt of irony from fucking Fortuna, Middlesbrough FC from the Premier League called. They had watched Kenneth for a while, and wanted to offer him a tree-year contract! Carly Rae Jepsen on full volume fit the situation perfectly:

Hey Kenneth
And this is crazy
But here's my number.
So call me, maybe?

But he didn't bloody call. And after doing some digging into my own self, I am assuming that it was something I said or did that made Kenneth stop calling me Jerry. Or something I didn't say or didn't do, that I may have promised him. There are always (at least) two points of views to a matter, and I am the first to admit that in this case it is definitely possible that the fault is on my side of the fence.

Several days passed, and rumours of Kenneth going to Lillestrøm appeared in the media. The Middlesbrough people called and asked me what the hell was going on. Did he chose Lillestrøm before them? Didn't this lad have any ambitions at all? They considered withdrawing the offer altogether; but I smoothed things out as best I could, and assured them that this was just the usual media nonsense. Of course, Kenneth wanted to go to England. But he still didn't answer my calls. So I sent all the info about the contact in England and what he needed to fix this himself, or cooperating with Tore Pedersen. I couldn't let a quarrel between us block an opportunity like this, even if I was pissed off and that's what I really wanted to do. Kenneth didn't care; he still chose Lillestrøm SK. The Middlesbrough people were not happy.

And I was enraged and furious with Kenneth. I called and texted him. After I threatened to kill him for the second time, he just replied, *"Don't ever contact me again!!"* The way I handled this situation was so pitiful, pathetic and un-manly that it is embarrassing just to think about it.

I am really sorry, Kenneth. Call me, maybe?

Kenneth flopped big time in Lillestrøm, by the way, and went back to Sogndal and later Brann.

I had become an experienced student in self-destructive behaviour, and my master's degree was right around the corner …

CURTAIN FALL

The usual bunch of childhood buddies were together for a party at Frank's place, in the same flat we used as our office a few years earlier. Frank and his missus were on the verge of breaking up for the second time at that point, so keeping the flat had turned out to be a good choice. These parties were always great fun. There were twelve of us, all guys, and we knew each other inside out. It was always relaxing; time off from wife and kids, and tipsy dives into ancient history. For a long time I considered writing a book about our childhood – it was really eventful – but being realistic I doubt it would have had many readers, and I do hope to get a little money out of it after having worked on this book for a year (*reviewers, please be nice to me*).

Late that night, and well down into the glasses, the display on my mobile told me that someone from abroad wanted my services. I had learned long time ago that not answering my phone can be expensive, regardless of the setting I'm in; it could be the one of fifty calls that potentially represented tens of thousands of euros. But it meant I also had to put up with the 49 of rubbish and fools. However, this was not rubbish; this was the 50th one.

It was the man from Trabzonspor calling; they were desperately looking for a forward, and they wanted to try a Norwegian one. He had watched a few matches here, not to mention that he was with me when Brann won the league championship – he had even seen me cry. No doubt, I was in good standing in his book, and I had his confidence. In other words, I was in a position where I could harvest some fruits of my relationship-building work; it was payday. The only thing I needed to do, was to come up with a name, a player I thought was good enough for them, and to a great extent he would believe my word. Trabzonspor should definitely not be sneered at. They put up five million euros flat for Stabæk's Brazilian player Alanzinho. A transfer like that could give as much as 5–600,000 euros in agent fees. Chances like this are the ones you wait for, and dream about. I knew very well who I could recommend – a forward that would make them very happy, and even at a reasonable price. However, the situation at that time was that I hadn't been quite online for the last months, so I decided on a somewhat unorthodox twist.

– *Give me twenty minutes, and I will call you back with a name. I just want to talk to the player first.*

– *Superb, Knut. Bye.*

Over the years, my friends had gotten used to me suddenly disappearing into a corner or another room to take a phone call, so they had no interest in what I was doing now. Stian was both the steadier and the biggest football fan of the lot. He was genuinely interested in my daily work, while the rest limited their interest to a high five the times I landed a big one. Absorbed in the atmosphere and laughter, I asked Stian if he wanted to play part in a stunt – if he could pretend to be a football player to a guy on the phone.

He is steady, but he is also equipped with a large dose of humour, so this was right up his alley of fun, and almost an hour after I hung up, we went into one of the bedrooms to call the Turk.

– *I have the perfect player for you, my friend. Sorry it took a while, but now I even have him with me here in my apartment.*

– *Fantastic. Give me his name, and I will check him out at soccerass.*

In the beginning of the 2000s, some really clever guys made a database over all professional football players in the world. That is, they made the framework for it. Then they established contacts in all countries, who were given the task of filling in all facts about clubs, players, matches, yellow cards and hundreds of other details, and it's continuously updated. With access to this database, you can quickly find any player and all relevant history about him; it has become the de-facto replacement of the traditional resume for football players. What used to be a hotchpotch of extremely untrustworthy resumes – a huge problem in the world of football – was now eliminated. And if you are a football player who are not

listed here, you can forget about playing on a higher level than
Division 7. All clubs, agents and scouts in the world use this
database, and access to it is pricy. These clever people have made a
really big business of it – kudos to you.

Now the Turk was signed in and ready to type in the name of
my incredible player in the search field.

– *His name is Stian Sætveit.* We covered the mic with our hands,
giggling.

The Turk didn't find anything, and asked me to spell his name.
Still nothing. I explained that there were Norwegian letters in the
name, which were different from how it is spelled in English – the
æ was usually rendered as e, a or ae. Nothing. The Turk was clearly
resigned – obviously, he was really excited about this player I had. I
gave the phone to Stian, and they exchanged a few words. When I
got the phone back, he said he felt it was a bit prematurely to
involve the player at this stage of the process. I apologised. *"No
problem, Knut."* Of course, I knew he would not find Stian on
SoccerAssociation; then a thought hit me.

– *Aaaah, I am so stupid. Sorry. Of course, he is not listed with the name
Stian Sætveit – that's the name the fans and media use, like a nickname. His
real name is Stig Johansen.*

I spelled it too. Stig appeared on his screen instantly, with a long
resume showing that he had been a loyal player for his club
Bodø/Glimt for many years. Many, many years.

Stian heard what came next – it was on speakerphone.

– *But Knut, are you fucking kidding me. Is THIS the guy you recommend
me?! He is almost 40 years old, man. Are you stupid?* Really angry now.

Two people can only keep their laughter trapped in their bellies
for so long – in the end it has to come out, and it did, at full
volume. When we got our breaths back, the only thing we heard
from the phone speaker was *biip biip biip biip.*

Wasting an opportunity like this was pure madness, and there
was no doubt that I was on a bad path and dangerously close to
rock bottom. The beginning of the end started a few months
earlier. Per-Ove, Roald and I had a great deal of success, and
collected several decent fees. We had landed transfers like Bojan
Zajic to Vålerenga, Ardian Gashi to Fredrikstad, Hassan El Fakiri
to Brann, Christian Kalvenes to Burnely, Rudolph Austin to Brann,
Nikola Djurdjic to Haugesund and Zsolt Korcsmar to Brann, in
addition to a bunch of smaller transfers that put bread and butter

on the table. We enjoyed the confidence of both our clients and our growing network abroad. Come to think of it, we had reached the perfect size, and we ought to have, in hindsight, been happy with what we had. But no – instead we started to mess around with a Danish agency who wanted us to join forces and become the largest agency in Scandinavia. The Danes were champions when it came to structure, branding and business modelling, and it all looked bloody impressive on paper. They had separate companies for business consulting for our clients, and a separate company for mental training, based on light hypnosis. Per-Ove and I even took a course to become hypnosis instructors, and it was a weird experience seeing Per-Ove lying on the bed desperately trying to be hypnotized by me. *"Fuck it, Knut, this is bullshit!"*

All the work in connection with the joint venture with the Danes was extremely expensive in terms of time, energy and money. In addition, the progress was slow as molasses. Early in the process, Roald and Per-Ove started to show their dislike of the entire plan, but I had enormous faith in this, so I pushed on, and promoted it to my two partners again and again. Even if they followed the plan loyally, they were clearly demotivated. They wanted to spend time on what they knew we were good at. Besides, we didn't have the means to go without income very long. I, on the other hand, felt I was being pulled in all directions, and had my hands full reassuring the Danes on one hand and the sceptics in my own camp on the other.

It was an extremely stressful period. We had had several meetings in Copenhagen, but now the Danes wanted to come to Bergen for a large and important meeting, like a founding convention. The subject of lot of the discussion between us was how to divide tasks and duties, how our common philosophy should be, establishing a common administration (something Per-Ove disliked intensely), not to mention an insanely complex system for distributing revenue. It described all possible scenarios. If a player were sold from Denmark to Holland, without any contribution from us in Norway, how much would we get? And if a player were sold between two Norwegian clubs, then what? Should a part of all the income go to a common fund to give us the possibility to expand later on? It was all a chaos of graphs, Excel sheets, percentages and so on. Which the Danes were really good at, as long as it could be displayed on a large screen with the aid of a projector. If those people had sold timeshare apartments on the Canary Islands, they could have retired after one season. I for one would definitely have signed and paid them for my two weeks a year on the island.

The convention in Bergen was drawing close, and a lot more people were invited than I had imagined. People from handball and ice hockey, in addition to football. Several Swedes were on the list, too, and a guy from Eastern Norway. I had received many instructions about what to prepare, and I was going to be the host of this two-day mini-convention. Per-Ove was sick and tired of the whole thing, and told me a few days before it was going down, that he did not bother to be part of this. I could run the meeting myself; he was staying home. In general Per-Ove didn't like this kind of happening, and with the Danes up to here, the choice was simple for him:

– *I call bullshit!*

Per-Ove was a million times more important to me than the Danes were, so I became really perplexed and upset. I couldn't just send an SMS to the pastry-eaters and tell them to call it off now. I was in deep shit – my own shit.

Moreover, I was light years behind the Danes when it came to arranging large meetings; I knew I wasn't anywhere near being prepared, and it stressed me out. The Danes too had spent lots of time and money on this; they would explode on me if I pulled the plug now. I really struggled to stay focused the last days before they arrived, while Per-Ove had retired completely from the project, and was instead running our shop while I was on out on thin ice.

The sum of the fear of losing Per-Ove and the fear of a collapse with the Danes, caused me to lose sleep. And it was on the nights before the convention in Bergen that I resorted to the bottle for the first time, to re-establish my inner calm. The movie from my D-day in Albania, with the blood-soaked sand, had its usual daily shows behind my eyelids. The intensity of the movie varied, but always increasing with my level of stress; it could be really bad in periods. During the first years, the movie had played exactly the same scene, over and over again. Four people outside a beach bar, all of them doing exactly the same things every time. However, four to five years after the incident – I don't remember exactly when I noticed for the first time – I could sometimes go in and make tiny changes in the way things happened; I became a sort of covert director. This mostly happened at night when I was trying to sleep, and the movie was absorbing all my attention. It was starting to give me a great sense of command over myself to be able to change the course of the film, not to mention its outcome. I also reduced the time I spent trying to fall asleep from no sleep on the worst days to an hour awake on the best. It was a strange and wonderful experience the first morning I woke up after spending only one hour falling asleep the night before.

Now, with the convention right around the corner, and an angry Ludvigsen, it was as if both cameraman, director and actors were on speed. The movie nights in bed were an intense hell, and sound was added to the worst scenes. It was so loud and realistic that I could swear others in the room had to hear it. However, the worst part was that I was deprived of all my rights as director – no control anymore.

The only thing left for me to do, was to ask for mercy from King Alcohol. He listened to his subject, and did his best to grant him peace. Although the day before the convention, it didn't do me any good to have a monarch on my team, even if I emptied an entire litre of his wonder liquid called Cognac.

The convention day was a hell of anxiety. I was sweating from every pore on my body, so you couldn't really see it on my light-blue shirt; it just became a shade darker and looked like it was made of an especially uncomfortable, body-clinging fabric. It went as it had to go, and to say the Danes were not impressed, is an understatement.

After this everybody were angry, and hassled me from all sides. Take a stand, Knut!

Take a stand, I? I could hardly cope with ordinary, day-to-day tasks. It was a living hell to keep a straight face to those around me, but I managed surprisingly well. However, not everyone was fooled by my act – not my brother. Take all sugar-coated stories about big brothers who are there for their little brothers. In The Brothers Lionheart, how touching isn't the love and sacrifice Karl's big brothers shows for him.

Jonatan – you are no match against my brother; he whacks both Tengil and Katla, simultaneously, with one arm on his back – before breakfast.

He kept me afloat; I knew that he knew. And he has his head put on the right way, my brother. The right words at the right time

– I've got your back, little brother.

I didn't take a proper stand; instead, I became an expert on kicking the can down the road and buying more time. And it sort of worked – for a while. Successful agent on the outside, liquid nerves on the inside.

For a long time I had challenged the limits of my psyche, and at last I didn't need to stretch them anymore; I was at breaking point. From that moment on, I have had the deepest respect for people who struggle with anxiety and related crap under their scalps.

A state of chaos; surviving on pure instinct; cold decisions; tough actions; sleepless nights with cramps.

The only straw I clung to, was being convinced that I couldn't fall deeper now. I had reached the bottom, and I was still alive, at least in the physical sense. Then the movie from the D-day gradually started to transform. Not the plot; it was still the same scene from hell. However, the characters switched places: the one who used to stand to the right just watching, was suddenly the active one. And this simple role swapping made the film, to put it a little childishly, a billion times worse to take in.

The shock in my body – the actual physical reaction – was monumental. In that moment when two plugs were connected inside my brain, I went into a state of complete, uncontrollable fear and anguish – full-blown anxiety. Two plugs that were pulled apart by the special forces in my own mind when the recordings of the film was made. They did it to spare me, my very own, considerate Delta Force. And they connected another plug, and made sure the manipulated movie was played for me a million times, trying to make me believe the new Director's Cut. Now the original version was back, the plan had failed, and I fell through the floor I believed was the basement a few moments ago.

Free fall. Curtain fall.

Until Rolf Barmen saved my life by crushing my world completely.

Rolf, today chairman of the board in SK Brann, is a man I count among my friends – a remote friend, but still a friend. He asked me out for dinner one night; said we needed to have a chat. He knew something. The piece of news he brought to the table, was of the highly dramatic sort; of the kind the scriptwriters of Hollyoaks would fume at, because even for them a plot like that would be too unbelievable. What Rolf told me, turned my personal life completely upside down, and was the start of my new way of life. Blood and honour, Rolf, blood and honour. Pure and simple.

For the last eighteen months, I had been dating a firework of a woman. Incredibly sexy, outgoing and wild. She fit my lifestyle perfectly. My friends, however, were a bit reluctant and reserved about her. My car-mad buddy Henrik put it in context. *"Sure, Knut, she is sexy as hell. But you can't drive a Ferrari every day. A Volkswagen is much better wife material."*

She lived in another city, and I had broken all the bank's and my own credit limits, and bought a house for well over 650,000 euros; I barely managed to service the loan. She had decorated the house and moved in, and I was there as often as I could, between my travelling domestically and abroad. Only weeks remained before I were going to bring all my stuff and live together with her on a permanent basis,

Rolf had friends in city I was moving to, and now he brought bad news, brutally delivered, no cute wrapping. Another man was living in my house; he had lived there for a while, but left the scene agilely every time I was there. Rolf's words hit me almost physically in my face. I became hot, my pulse accelerating. Panic hit me before I even had time to feel any anger. There were so many aspects to this. The betrayal, of course – it sucked big time in itself. Then the degradation and humiliation; the thought of everyone soon finding out. Then a very real economic fear. I was in my neck to shit with this house, and she was living in it. However, Rolf did a great job delivering this news, as he often does. He is a wise man.

But when I got up from bed the next day, after yet another sleepless night, the cocktail of feelings from the night before had been replaced with a white, blinding rage; pure survival instinct. I got a flight out of Bergen the same morning. Before take-off, I called her, without sharing what I learned the day before, only to inform her that I was on my way: ... *so it would be great if you could be home at around four.* During a stopover, I bought a tape recorder. I wanted to tape the conversation I was about to have in a few hours; my entire economic future was at stake.

As I stepped into my house, I went straight to the point. Surprisingly my voice and tone sounded completely normal. I spoke clearly and for a long time, despite her persistent attempts to say something. My torrent ended in a series of demands. I gave her a half hour to pack her clothes and other necessities. To my relief she put all her cards on the table straight away, and she seemed genuinely despairing. She said it had started little by little, and that she had meant to tell me. I couldn't care less. After having packed her things silently, she came down to the kitchen to me, and made a whole-hearted attempt to clear the air. She tried with one of those smiles I would normally have loved; her body a little slanted, one foot pulled a bit up against her calf, slanted, naughty smile with a slight biting of her lips. That used to be the first hint of a pleasant time. Now it glanced off. For the first time in my life, I really understood what people mean when they say that they feel completely emotionally void. I was cold.

I rarely get angry, and she had never seen that side of me; but when I do lose my temper, I don't catch fire; I explode. She was taken by surprise by my violent rage, and left the house crying, out to the car of a friend of hers who was waiting.

I locked the door and dumped exhausted down in the coach. *Now what?* After two days and one night without sleeping, with my body in constant tension, I fell asleep. I didn't wake up until late the same evening, and I could see on my mobile that she had called me several times.

I called her back, and understood immediately from her voice that she was in another mode than when she left the house. With two girl friends in the background, jazzing her up, she had found her inner warrior. She wouldn't bloody well put up with this, and demanded to move back into the house; quoted law, and threatened me with this and that. She accepted to a certain degree that since I owned the house, I alone could decide whether to sell it or not. But after all, a house sale could take time, maybe months, and she demanded to live there in the meantime. Evening turned into night, and the only thing we managed to agree on, was to call each other the next day.

Early next morning I called a lawyer in Oslo that my family had used for years. I updated him on my situation, and his advice was clear: Do not let her move back in! According to the current laws, that would most likely mean that I had to go through a difficult and potentially prolonged process. He recommended me to change the locks, in case she had a copy of the key, and he also mentioned that I should hand over to her every single item in the house that was hers.

— If you have the opportunity, Knut, I strongly recommend that you live in

the house until things settle down. To put it simply, it's the one on the inside of the house that has the upper hand, no matter what the law says.

I hung up, both relieved and stressed. I decided to call the broker through whom I had bought the house. We had become well acquainted in the process, since he had done a formidable effort towards both the bank and the sellers to make this purchase became reality. After all, I had in reality water over my head with this house.

I told him all the gritty details, and was aware that he was the very first one I told; I felt the embarrassment. However, he had consideration and empathy, and was solution-oriented. An hour later, the locksmith was at my door, and installed an innovative lock with no keys – only a fingerprint scanner. The real estate broker arrived, and I asked him to scan his finger as well, to have access to the house. He was going to start the process of finding a buyer immediately. One problem remained: I couldn't stay in the house. I had important meetings in Montenegro the next day and in Germany later the same week. What the fuck do I do?

I called a childhood friend, Martin. He became the first in my circle that I told; it was still embarrassing. Before I managed to collect myself and formulate a question, he said, *"I'm on the next flight to your place."*

Five hours later the taxi stopped outside, and Martin entered. A friendly hug of the really good kind, hard and long; no words. At last, for the first time since my dinner with Rolf, the tears came – cascading. Martin took two weeks off from work, and stayed in the house. He packed her things, arranged them to be delivered, and after consulting with the broker he painted walls and cleaned the entire house so it was ready for showing and sale. Martin, as Paris Hilton says, *"You are my BFF – best friend forever."*

According to the graph on the home page of Statistics Norway, real estate prices had increased gradually month by month for twelve years – a total of 144 months. I bought my house on the hundred and forty-fifth month, at the peak of the graph. Then the line turned to an uncomfortably abrupt decline from the 146th week and onwards. My real estate broker did a man's job in a market that was heavy as lead, but I ended up having to accept a loss of 125,000 euros.

Combined with an agent career out of control and an even worse mental state, I was rapidly approaching total collapse and personal bankruptcy.

By now, everybody at home knew what had happened, and it wasn't embarrassing anymore. People tend to share their own experiences in situations like this. My mum insisted that I should go and see a doctor; this wasn't just going to fix itself. So I got an appointment with my doctor. I had seen him four to five times before, with trivial matters like ear infections, simple fractions and constipation. Doctor Selim is from Egypt, and passionately engaged in football, so we usually end up talking more about football than the reason for my visit. He always talks warmly about Egyptian football players, who he thinks are grossly underrated. Besides he is a macho man, and expects me to act like one too – no frills or 'poor you' from him. His book of medical certificates was collecting dust in a drawer. Not that a sick leave would do me any good. You cannot just stop your work for a month when you are an agent – it doesn't work like that. Therefore, when I came to him with a non-physical condition, he was almost embarrassed.

– *You are a man, Knut, you just have to swallow this and work your way through it. I cannot do anything to help you.*

I explained again, in more detail, how I could not sleep, about my anxiety and the attacks of sweating I was having.

In the psychologist's sofa the next day, I was well into the process of getting it all off my chest. I had decided not to wrap up anything; I would just be as honest as possible, and wait for the expert's qualified judgement. She listened carefully to the story about my experiences in Albania and how they had resurfaced lately. After the session, she said plainly that this was outside her field of expertise and experience. She recommended me to try to get a session at the Centre for Crisis Psychology. They specialised in war veterans, victims of violence and rape, and other forms of posttraumatic stress.

I called the centre, but no good news from them. They had a long waiting time – up to four months – and nothing would be reimbursed, so the treatment would be very expensive. I told them I wanted them to add me to their waiting list. I was pleasantly surprised when they called me a week later: if I would accept a slightly non-standard approach, they could offer me help. They had a newly qualified psychologist I could go to; this would be a part of her education and training, and usually be conducted with an experienced psychologist present as well, for quality assurance of the treatment. I was in.

The apprentice was a stunningly beautiful woman in her mid-twenties, so it felt a bit awkward opening up to her. However, she was good at what she did, so during the third session I released all constraints. Oh, Lord!

A few days later, I was standing on the outside of a building where I had an important meeting. I was smoking a cigarette and turned around a bit so I could see the bank building next to it. This was my favourite branch, where I always went if I needed some qualified assistance beyond what you can normally get online. For instance when I juggled an amount of hundreds of thousands to the Balkans, destined for clubs, players, investors and tax authorities. They had very skilled people in that bank. I was hoping the case handler I was about to meet was equally skilled, and I put out my cigarette before entering the double doors under the three red letters: NAV – the acronym for the Norwegian Labour and Welfare Administration.

After having read countless stories in the media about people in despair from cruel and unjust treatment from NAV, it was with a certain unease and almost fear I went to meet my caseworker. But what a man! He put all critical mentions to shame, and there is no doubt that he was one of the key people who helped me to get me up on my feet again. You don't often see positive stories like that in the media, but do I hope there are many more of them out there.

– *Well, well, Knut*, I told myself as I lit another cigarette out on the pavement after the meeting.

– *In like a lion, out like a lamb; the times of plenty have come to an end.*

EPILOGUE

Ullevaal business class, September 2006. It is five to ten – five to exam – and I am waiting for an extremely important phone call. Vlado promised me he would call at half past nine; I am completely stressed out!

After failing miserably on my first exam in March, I realized that I needed to do something new to pass in September. I thought a lot about this, but didn't come up with any obvious solutions. Except cramming, of course, and hope for a bit of good luck. The thought of cheating had crossed my mind several times, but there wasn't any easy way to do that, except for browsing through the book during the exam without being caught. I could just as well forget about it.

When I went to watch the World Cup in Germany in June that year, I still hadn't come up with any plan, and I was kicking the can further down the road. Vlado and I quickly became good friends, and a late night at Roberto's restaurant towards the end of the World Cup, I mentioned my concern regarding the exam to Vlado. He nodded understandingly, and admitted he had been through the same – he had failed the exam. So, Vlado didn't have the license either.

He too had enrolled for September, and this time he was certain he was going to pass.

– How can you be so sure, Vlado? I am not getting any wiser, no matter how much I cram.

– *Because, Knut* … – smiling, before he took a long sip of the

Brunello, pausing deliberately – *because I already have the answers.*

Big grin and a wonderful laughter.

How the hell could he have the answers? They were guarded literally like state secrets. No associations were allowed to see neither the questions nor the answers until thirty minutes before the start of the exam, and then only one person per association – the secretary.

Good old Roberto had overheard our conversation and came over to our table. He put his hand lightly on my shoulder and smiled.

– *No problem, Kenute,* as many non-Norwegians pronounce my name. *You are my friend. I will help you.*

They had bought a co-worker in one of the associations for 20,000 euros, and they were originally three people who should be sharing the intel. Now I was offered a ticket to heaven against paying a fourth of the bill – 5000 euros. Pocket change considering what it got me.

Our bought and paid for co-worker received the fax half an hour before the exam started, so there was no time to lose getting the information out to all four of us.

Therefore, I am standing on Ullevaal, sweating, when my phone rings one minute to ten. After an agitated start of the conversation, Vlado takes control. He is, like myself, standing outside an exam room in another country, while the rest of the candidates are already sitting in their chairs.

– *Knut, just write down the letters. Are you ready?*

Frantically I reach for the *Hurtigruta Carglass* pen and a brown napkin.

– *Come on, Vlado. I am ready. Hurry!!*

– *A, A, B, D, A, B, C, C, B, D, A, A, D, C, C. That's all.*

I hang up and run into the room where the other candidates are already seated, ready to start the exam, while apologizing deeply and sincerely to the secretary as I enter sideways between her and the door she is closing…

TO THE SHERIFF OF NOTTINGHAM

I would like to make a statement to the Tax Collection Office, if the tax collector can find a minute in his or her busy schedule: all funds I have received during my agent career are declared and paid tax for.

Cross my heart and hope to die.

If, God Almighty forbid, some of it was off the books, it has of course been in the form of cash, and is therefore very difficult to remember. Most of it was probably used on alcohol and cigarettes, thus the lion's share of it ended up right back to the state administration anyway through applicable dues and taxes. Case closed.

POSTSCRIPT

Dear Reader! It makes me happy to know that you've got this far – it probably means you didn't think the book sucked. Or maybe you were bored on an airport while waiting for the Dreamliner to start boarding, and this book was all you had to pass the time. Whatever the reason, if you have read this book, you have my kudos. My already inflated ego may become unbearable by the fact that people pay tens of euros to read my writings. I will just have to manage that as best I can without driving people around me insane by constantly checking online for any comments about my book. Gollum.

The book ends dramatically. And it was dramatic. During your reading you have probably realized that I didn't use much filtering when writing, especially not the parts about myself. To be able to believe my story, you need the whole truth and nothing but the truth – not just scattered bits and pieces of it.

Needless to say, I hope the book sells massively, and for two reasons – both purely selfish ones: firstly to earn money, of course, which I need like the rest of the world; and secondly for the recognition I am going to feel by people reading and liking what I have written. If I miss on both those points – if the book flops and my readers hate it – I honestly admit that I am going to feel a bit stupid. I know I have put my head on the block with this book, and that can go both ways. I have undressed completely, and it would be sad if nobody even found it interesting.

Anyway, time will tell, and I am very grateful that you read this book. Even if it's just you, Mum.

I can't deny that it took some time before I was back on my feet. And if you care, I can tell you my life is very good now, and has been so for several years. After spending hundreds of days a year travelling when I was an agent, I got my fill of glam and living in a suitcase. Now I live a short distance from Bergen, on an abandoned farm I have refurbished together with my fiancée Lena, my daughter Julie and my "bonus" daughter Iselin. I work eight to four in charge of large accounts in an accessories company – ballpoint pen salesman, as I say if anybody asks. This is a job where I can put all my work in a mental drawer at five o'clock. Strongly recommended.

We also have a herd of wild sheep and a few ducks. Truly a wonderful life.

I know how to sell football players and ballpoint pens. Now I can slaughter sheep too.

I definitely know how to fall on my face, and how to get back up again.

What more can an alley cat from Bergen want from life?

AN ACKNOWLEDGEMENT WORTH READING

A fulfilling and exciting life with plenty of madness isn't possible without lots of fabulous people around you. There are almost an infinite number of people who mean a lot to me, who deserve their acknowledgement for one thing or another, but I only have room here for the ones who have contributed to this book.

Thanks to my buddies who let me include them in this book, especially Erlend, Daniel and Frank. Hope your divorce doesn't end up costing you too much, Frank. For Daniel, the incident in Poland was just like another Monday in his life, so not many people will raise their eyebrows over that. Thank you Erlend for being part of the book, and a special thank you for the years you have been my close friend, great neighbour and good football buddy. Thank you for reading eagerly and for your valuable feedback in the process. And, of course, thanks to you, Stian, for contributing details about the phone call to Turkey, when you, as usual, had the lower blood-alcohol level of the two of us. A special thanks to Meyer who, despite a rough period of illness in his own life, took the time to read and motivate me. My brother from another mother, Eilif, who insisted you didn't want as much as a hint of yourself in the book (understandably), thank you for your words of wisdom. My dentist friend, Anders, who keeps enjoying the cinnamon buns I bring him, while waiting for the anaesthetic to kick in. And thanks to all you guys for your enthusiasm and good contributions. You know damn well who you are!

Thank you to my hunting friend and neighbour Ludvig, who is good at keeping me on the ground when I get high on myself, and his extraterrestrially wonderful wife who cut my hair so nicely before I went to the publishing party at Kagge.

Thanks to Bjarte L. and Per Magne for good contributions, and to Frode, who makes sure my sheep get hay while I am inside writing.

Mum and dad, to both of you for everything you mean to me. Brother.

Thanks to father-in-law and Michael, both full-blooded Brann supporters. Steffen.

My dear Lena, who must love to care for this strange man. Iselin, my "bonus" daughter who I know dig me, although I'm right there in the doorway with the shotgun when you bring home scoundrels. I dig you too. My genetical masterpiece, Julie. Everybody knows what someone like you mean to someone like me. Sob.

Thank you, Jannikke, for the handsome front page photo. Thanks to my ballpoint pen boss, Endre.

Thank you to Morten S, Lars L and Kristin for fabulous and crucial consultancy. The woman I both love and hate, my editor Tuva, thank you for everything you have done in this process, and that's quite a bit. And to your colleagues and fellow warriors in the publishing house – the budding agent Thomas; Jens (who constantly gets sent out from meetings); Raymond, the jovial strategist; exuberant Anne – and of course, thank you to the man who is paying for this rubbish, Kagge himself.

Finally, a special and warm thanks to my fantastic translator Bjorn, his consultant Louise, and his brother Einar, who made it possible for you guys to read an English version of this book.

ABOUT THE AUTHOR

Knut Høibraaten is a former football agent, now ballpoint pen salesman and sheep farmer in Samnanger, a neighbouring parish of Bergen, Norway. He was born and grew up in Bergen, where he developed a strong love and passion for the football club Brann and an absorbing interest in football in general.